a taste of spring

Mindy Heiferling

a taste of spring

recipes to celebrate the season

Illustrations by Melanie Marder Parks

Clarkson Potter/Publishers

New York

To my mother, who taught me how to live, and my father, who taught me how to eat.

The information about wild mushrooms originally appeared in *Food & Wine* magazine in slightly different form. Grateful acknowledgment is made to *Food & Wine* magazine for permission to reprint it.

Published by Clarkson N. Potter, Inc., 201 East 50th Street, New York, New York, 10022. Member of the Crown Publishing Group. Random House, Inc. New York, Toronto, London, Sydney, Auckland

CLARKSON N. POTTER, POTTER, and colophon are trademarks of Clarkson N. Potter, Inc.

Manufactured in Hong Kong

Library of Congress Cataloging-in-Publication Data
Heiferling, Mindy
A taste of spring / by Mindy Heiferling.
Includes index
1. Cookery, American. I. Title
TX715.H417 1993
647.9573—dc20   92-14705 CIP

ISBN 0-517-59016-6
10 9 8 7 6 5 4 3 2 1
First Edition

a c k n o w l e d g m e n t s

Many people, each in his or her own way, helped make this book possible—and a pleasure to write. I am very grateful to them.

My friends and family, for their love and faith in me. Bob Hoebee, for his inspiration and friendship. Pam Krauss, my editor, for believing in me and being such a joy to work with. Judith Weber, my agent, fellow ex-Brooklynite and Italophile, for her perseverance, enthusiasm, and wise counsel. Katie Workman, for her enthusiasm and unswerving support. Kelly Kochendorfer, for keeping me laughing and for eating my shad roe. Shelley Boris, for helping me to become a better cook, sometimes in spite of myself. Sally Schneider, for her friendship, generosity of spirit, and poetic musings on ramps. Edward Amber, for getting me started. Rose Marie Laster, Geri Brin, Susan Wyler, Marya Dalrymple, Tanya Wenman, and Pamela Mitchell, for helping me to become a better writer. Irena Chalmers, for being a great role model. The editorial staff at *Food & Wine*, for their continuing encouragement.

And for their invaluable information on ingredients, I am indebted to the following individuals: Jim Caito and Gene Mattiuzzo of Caito Fisheries, Joseph Enea of Pisacane Midtown, Joan Garvin of DeBragga & Spitler, John Gottfried of Metro AgriBusiness, the knowledgeable butchers at Jefferson Market, Wendy Krupnick of Shepherd's Garden Seeds, Stanley Osczepinski, farmer, Anita Richards of the Lamb Co-Op, and Priscilla Root of the American Lamb Council.

Thanks also go to the many cookbook authors whose work continues to inspire and excite me: Julia Child, Paula Wolfert, James Beard, Marcella Hazan, Madeleine Kamman, Giuliano Bugialli, Marion Cunningham, Margaret Fox, Alice Waters, Edna Lewis, Elizabeth David, John Thorne, Elizabeth Schneider, Joyce Goldstein, Richard Sax and Sandra Gluck, and Lidia Bastianich.

contents

introduction

Spring, for me, has always been the happiest of seasons, signaling, more than any other time of the year, promise. It means that cold, dark wintertime, when I have to don endless layers of clothing to brave the elements, is over, and I have much to look forward to—months of warmer weather, flowers and trees in bloom, longer days, and the pleasures of cooking and eating all the wonderful things that the earth brings forth as it warms up.

In New York, where I live, I can get just about any spring food all year long—asparagus from Mexico, apricots from Chile, rhubarb from Holland, cherries from New Zealand. Perhaps I should consider myself lucky to have access to such things whenever I care to, but the idea of buying strawberries in the dead of winter (and at exorbitant prices) seems a bit skewed to me.

I feel that food tastes best in its own season and don't mind waiting for the first asparagus from California or the first ramps from West Virginia to make their appearance in local markets; in fact, these are things I look forward to during our harsh, soul-chilling winters. I know that in a few short months these vegetables will be gone, replaced by the tomatoes and sweet corn of summer, and that's fine. Food seems more special when I realize that it's only available for a brief time, and I see this as a challenge to myself as a cook. I look at what's available at the produce markets and fish stands and let whatever is freshest and best be the inspiration for my meals.

This book is a guide to the various foods that are seasonal in the spring, with information and recipes for each to enlighten, and I hope, inspire you to create some lovely spring meals on your own.

Eggs In recent years, incidents of salmonella poisoning have been on the rise. To kill the salmonella bacteria, the U.S. government warns against preparations using raw or partly cooked eggs. Two recipes in this book—Cold Shad with Artichoke and Olive Sauce and Cold Asparagus with Watercress-Orange Mayonnaise—contain raw eggs. You can substitute commercial mayonnaise in these two recipes, bearing in mind that the flavor will be somewhat different.

My own way of dealing with the risk of salmonella is to buy only free-range eggs (salmonella is largely the result of poor sanitation in large commercial chicken farms), keep them refrigerated, and discard any with cracks. When I make mayonnaise, I follow a salmonella-killing procedure recommended by a food scientist in *The New York Times* (but not, I must add, endorsed by the USDA): I let the egg yolks sit for 10 minutes with the vinegar or lemon juice used in the recipe, before adding the oil.

Cream I use only fresh, pasteurized (but not ultra-pasteurized) heavy cream in cooking for two reasons: It tastes better and the ultra-pasteurized type, because it has been stabilized through long pasteurization, does not reduce to the thick consistency necessary for sauces.

Fresh Herbs The more I cook, the more I realize how much the flavor intensity and nuances of all fresh foods, not just herbs, can vary. Basil, for example, can be sweet and mild or harsh and anisey, and the only way to tell is to taste it. The quantities of herbs in my recipes are guidelines; taste before you cook, and use more or less, as you see fit. Don't be afraid to trust your palate.

spring *seafood and lamb*

Though I can–and do–buy salmon year-round, in spring I like to cook salmon with the seasonal vegetables that taste so good with it, such as asparagus and small potatoes, and with lighter-tasting herbs and seasonings like chives and tarragon. I celebrate shad and soft-shell crabs similarly, keeping the approach light yet satisfying and choosing complementary spring herbs and vegetables to enhance them.

I love lamb most of all in the spring, and emphasize its flavor with a light approach. I prepare it with red wine, lemon mint, orange, rosemary, or thyme, and combine it with seasonal vegetables like artichokes or baby carrots.

The recipes in this section range from light brunch or luncheon offerings to savory stews–all of them redolent of the flavors of spring.

s a l m o n

With its pretty peach color and delicate flavor, salmon seems perfectly suited to springtime menus. It also marries well with other spring foods, such as asparagus, peas, fiddlehead ferns, ramps, new potatoes, and greens.

All wild salmon are anadromous, meaning that they are born in freshwater lakes or streams, go to the sea, where they spend most of their lives, and then return to their birthplace to spawn. Most wild salmon are caught in the ocean or in river mouths before they have begun to spawn, at which time their natural reserves of fats and oils are highest and they are thus at their most flavorful. More than 90 percent of the commercial catch in the United States comes from Alaska, with the rest coming from Washington, Oregon, and California. Six species of salmon are commonly sold here; of these, king, or Chinook, and coho are at their best in the spring months.

King salmon are the largest (usually around forty pounds) of the five Pacific salmons, with the highest oil content (about 15 percent of their body weight), which gives them a rich flavor and buttery texture. The flesh of king salmon, which are prized for their wild flavor, ranges in color from white to deep orange. Their season generally runs from May to late September.

Coho (silver) salmon, with deep-colored flesh, usually weigh six to twelve pounds and are leaner than king, with an oil content that ranges from 2 to 12 percent. Their season is shorter than that of king, beginning June 1 and ending whenever the government's predetermined quota has been reached. Excellent baby coho salmon, the size of trout, are now being farm-raised on the West Coast and in Chile; they are available throughout the year, boned and butterflied like trout.

Salmon's flavor is best complemented by herbs that won't overwhelm, particularly parsley, chives, chervil, tarragon, and thyme.

Buying Criteria When buying any kind of fresh fish, choose your market carefully. The fish should be sitting on or partly covered by chopped ice. When selecting whole fish, look for shiny skin, bright red (not brownish) gills, clear eyes that are not sunken in their sockets, and firm flesh that springs back from your touch. Fillets and steaks should look moist, without any separations in the flesh (except, with fillets, in the areas where the pinbones have been removed). Fresh fish will smell faintly of the sea but should never smell "fishy." For the moistest fish, buy fillets that have been cut from the head or center of the salmon, rather than the tail.

To Prepare for Cooking Salmon, whether whole or in fillets or steaks, is sold ready to cook. Fillets, however, often need to have the pinbones (on either side of the spine, near the head) removed. This is easily done: holding the flesh down with one hand, grasp a pinbone firmly with tweezers or pliers and pull it out in the direction in which it is pointing. Repeat until all of the pinbones have been removed. Many people, myself included, take some sort of perverse pleasure in removing pinbones, not finding it tedious in the least.

Sautéed Baby Coho Salmon
with Herbed Cucumber Sauce

4 servings

This is a wonderfully easy dish to make for a spring lunch or dinner. Make the sauce at least one hour before you plan to eat, but be sure to eat it on the same day; otherwise, the cucumbers tend to get watery and the chives assume an "off" flavor.

Herbed Cucumber Sauce
½ cup plus 1 tablespoon crème fraîche (see Note)
¼ cup finely diced Kirby cucumber
2 tablespoons snipped chives
2 teaspoons finely chopped fresh chervil
1 tablespoon finely chopped celery leaves
Salt and freshly ground black pepper

1 tablespoon unsalted butter
1 tablespoon olive oil

Combine all of the sauce ingredients in a small bowl. Cover and refrigerate for at least 1 hour to allow the flavors to develop.

Heat the butter and oil in a 10-inch skillet over medium heat. Meanwhile, lightly coat two of the salmon on both sides with flour. When the fat is hot, add the salmon and cook for 3 minutes, turning once, until cooked through and lightly golden, seasoning with the salt and pepper as they cook. Keep warm in a slow (150° F.) oven. Repeat with the two remaining salmon, adding a little more butter and oil if needed, and drain on paper towels.

4 baby Coho salmon (8 to 10 ounces each), boned and butterflied
Flour for dredging
Salt and freshly ground black pepper

Serve the salmon with the sauce on the side.

Note: You may substitute sour cream thinned with a little heavy cream for the crème fraîche.

Fresh Salmon Cakes
with Deep-Fried Celery Leaves

4 entree or 8 appetizer servings

While researching an article on mail-order dinners for a magazine, I ordered some crab cakes from Faidley Seafood in Baltimore and found them to be incredible—light, yet packed with richly flavored crabmeat. This recipe, a salmon version of Faidley's crab cakes, is similarly delicate, with scallions, tarragon, and celery leaves accenting the subtle flavor of the salmon.

Preheat the oven to 400° F.

Rub the salmon with the olive oil, season with the salt and pepper, and bake for 8 minutes, until cooked about three-quarters of the way through. Discard the skin and bones, flake the flesh, and set aside to cool.

While the salmon cools, heat the butter in a small skillet and add the scallion. Cook over medium heat for 5 minutes, stirring often, until the scallion softens. Transfer to a small bowl and stir in the tarragon.

In a medium bowl, whisk together the mayonnaise and egg. Stir in the Saltine crumbs and let sit for 5 minutes.

Drain off any juices that may have accumulated around the fish and gently fold it into the crumb mixture, along with the scallion and tarragon. Season with salt and pepper. Form into eight 3-inch cakes, put onto a plate lined with wax paper, cover, and chill for 2 hours.

Preheat the broiler.

Transfer the salmon cakes to a lightly oiled broiler pan and cook on the lower shelf of the broiler for 5 minutes, turning once, until lightly browned. Keep warm.

While the cakes cook, heat ½ inch of vegetable oil to 375° F. in a small saucepan. Add the celery leaves carefully, in batches if necessary, and cook for 20 seconds, until crisp. With a slotted spoon, transfer to paper towels to drain. Sprinkle with kosher salt.

2 salmon steaks (about 1 pound each)
1 teaspoon olive oil
Salt and freshly ground black pepper to taste
1 tablespoon unsalted butter
⅔ cup chopped scallion, white and light green parts with a bit of dark green
1½ teaspoons chopped fresh tarragon
3 tablespoons plus 1 teaspoon mayonnaise
1 large egg
¼ cup low-salt Saltine crumbs
Vegetable oil for deep-frying
1½ cups celery leaves, rinsed and dried well (see Note)
Kosher salt
Lemon wedges

Put the salmon cakes on plates, sprinkle with the celery leaves, and garnish with lemon wedges.

Note: When buying the celery for this recipe, be sure to choose a head that has a generous proportion of leaves.

Warm Composed Salad with Grilled Salmon, Leeks, Asparagus, and Tiny Potatoes

2 servings

Although this dish has a lot of steps, it's really very easy to prepare, and if you want to serve it at room temperature, the various components can be cooked ahead of time, at whatever pace you like. Just don't refrigerate before serving.

Put the tarragon, chives, and oil into a food processor and process for 30 seconds, until the herbs are finely chopped and the oil takes on a green color. Strain through a medium sieve, pressing with a wooden spoon to extract all the flavor. In a small bowl, whisk the vinegar and mustard with the salt and pepper until blended. Slowly whisk in the flavored oil until the vinaigrette emulsifies.

Tarragon-Chive Vinaigrette
2 teaspoons chopped fresh tarragon
3 tablespoons chopped chives
½ cup fruity olive oil
2 tablespoons sherry vinegar
¼ teaspoon Dijon mustard
Salt and freshly ground black pepper

Preheat the broiler.

Bring 1 inch of salted water to a boil in a medium skillet. Leaving a small portion of the root ends attached, trim the roots and dark green tops, cut the leeks in half lengthwise, and rinse well to remove all grit. Add the leeks to the skillet, cover, and simmer for 10 minutes, until just tender. Drain well on paper towels. Brush the leeks with 2 tea-

2 medium leeks

8 tiny red potatoes (about 6 ounces, total), scrubbed and halved, or 4 larger potatoes cut in quarters

1 teaspoon kosher salt

4 asparagus spears, trimmed and cut diagonally into 1-inch pieces

2 salmon fillets (4 to 5 ounces each), skin removed

Salad

1 cup watercress, tough stems removed

1 cup Bibb, Boston, or oak-leaf lettuce leaves

2 teaspoons snipped fresh chives

1 teaspoon finely chopped fresh tarragon

spoons of the vinaigrette and broil until flecked with brown, about 3 minutes, turning once.

Meanwhile, place the potatoes in a saucepan with cold water to cover by 1 inch. Add the salt and bring to a simmer, then cover and cook for 10 minutes, until tender. Drain in a colander, refresh with cold running water, and dry with paper towels. In a small bowl, toss the potatoes with 2 teaspoons of the vinaigrette.

Cook the asparagus until crisp-tender in a pot of rapidly boiling salted water. Drain, refresh, and dry as with the potatoes, and toss in another bowl with about 2 teaspoons of the vinaigrette.

Brush the salmon on both sides with a little of the vinaigrette and grill or broil about 4 inches from the heat, turning once, for 6 minutes, just until the white globules of fat rise to the surface of the fish. Let the salmon cool slightly.

Toss the greens with some of the vinaigrette and divide between two plates. Put the salmon in the center of each plate and arrange the vegetables around it. Combine the chives and tarragon and sprinkle over the salmon and vegetables.

s h a d

The first time I ever ate shad was about twenty years ago, when I cooked a recipe for shad fillets Doria that appeared in *The New York Times*. This classic French preparation combines herbed, battered fillets that are sautéed, then finished in cream and garnished with fried bread cubes and sautéed cucumber ovals. A bit fussy by today's standards, but it was utterly delicious, and I've been a shad aficionado ever since.

Shad is the largest member of the herring family and, like salmon, is anadromous, spending most of its life in the ocean and returning to the inland rivers of its birth to spawn. While shad are indigenous to the East Coast, they are now found on the West Coast as well, thanks to the efforts of a fish culturist named Seth Green, who in 1871 transported shad fry (recently hatched shad) to California and released them into the Sacramento River.

Atlantic shad begin their spawning run as early as December, but the peak season, when flavor is best, supply is most abundant, and prices are lowest, is March through May. The season starts in Florida and progresses up the coast to Canada as the waters warm up. On the West Coast, peak shad season is May through July.

Shad's high oil content gives it a moist texture and rich flavor that is somewhere between trout and bluefish. Because shad has more than 350 bones, it is almost always sold in fillets that have been boned by specialists (though I knew one poor soul who, unaware of shad's bone structure, bought a whole one at a market in Chinatown). There are recipes for whole shad, which call for long cooking to soften the bones. Whole shad are also planked, Native

American–style—that is, attached to a wooden board and cooked over an open fire. In fact, residents near many coastal rivers down South celebrate the season with shad plankings or bakes. I'm happy just to eat the fillets, fried, baked, or broiled. Shad tastes best when treated simply, flavored with mild herbs like parsley, scallions, chives, bay leaves, and thyme.

Buying Criteria Shad fillets should look moist. The flesh will, of course, be broken in various spots where the bones have been removed.

To Prepare for Cooking Shad fillets may be cooked whole, but as they tend to be tricky to turn because of the separations in the flesh, I often cut them into strips along the lines of separation.

Cornmeal-Crusted Shad
with Tomato Vinaigrette

4 servings

Quick to make, this dish, like just about any fried fish, is great with coleslaw. For optimal flavor, the vinaigrette should be made 1 hour in advance.

To make the vinaigrette, halve the tomatoes, squeeze out the seeds and juice, and cut each half in half again to make wedges. Put in the work bowl of a food processor and process for a few seconds, until chopped fine. Add the salt and pepper to taste, and the vinegar, and process to blend. With the motor running, add the oil in a slow stream until the mixture has emulsified. Stir in the remaining ingredients, adding a bit of sugar if the tomatoes seem overly acidic.

Tomato Vinaigrette
2 ripe plum tomatoes
Salt and freshly ground
  black pepper
1 tablespoon plus 1 tea-
  spoon balsamic vinegar
¼ cup fruity olive oil
1 scant teaspoon chopped
  fresh flat-leaf parsley
1 scant teaspoon chopped
  fresh marjoram
1 small garlic clove,
  minced
Tiny dash cayenne
Tiny pinch sugar, if needed

To prepare the shad, beat the egg in a shallow dish and put the cornmeal on a sheet of wax paper. Dip the fillets in the egg, then in the cornmeal; season with the salt and pepper. Put the fillets on a rack set on a

Shad

1 large egg
¾ cup yellow or white cornmeal
4 shad fillets (about 6 ounces each)
Salt and freshly ground black pepper
½ cup safflower oil
1 tablespoon unsalted butter

plate and refrigerate, uncovered, for at least 20 minutes to set the breading.

Heat the oil and butter in a large skillet over medium-high heat. When the fat is very hot, add the fillets, skin-side down. Lower the heat to medium and cook, turning once, for about 8 minutes, until deep golden.

Serve the shad hot, with the Tomato Vinaigrette.

Cold Shad with Artichoke
and Olive Sauce

8 servings

I love this Mediterranean-flavored sauce, which is good with any number of things, including other types of fish (try it with salmon, tuna, or swordfish) and steamed new potatoes, and as a dip for crudités. When I created this recipe I ended up disproving Nora Ephron's contention (in her funny book Heartburn) *that anything that tastes good with capers tastes better without them—an axiom with which I've generally agreed, I hasten to add. I first made this sans capers but found that it needed some oomph. The dreaded capers not only provided that but somehow magically brought out the elusive artichoke flavor, as well. Serve this chilled or at room temperature.*

Shad
8 shad fillets (about 6 ounces each)
1 tablespoon olive oil
Salt and freshly ground black pepper

Preheat the oven to 450° F.

Brush the shad all over with the oil and season with salt and pepper. Put on a baking sheet and bake for 8 minutes, until cooked through. Cover and refrigerate, if desired, or let it stand at room temperature.

To make the sauce, put the artichoke hearts, garlic, and mustard in the work bowl of a food processor and process for a few seconds,

Artichoke and Olive Sauce

½ cup canned marinated
    artichoke hearts or Oven-
    Braised Artichokes (page
    49)
½ teaspoon chopped garlic
½ teaspoon Dijon mustard
2 large egg yolks, at room
    temperature
2 tablespoons fresh lemon
    juice
2 tablespoons chopped
    pitted Niçoise or Gaeta
    olives
1 tablespoon nonpareil
    capers
1 tablespoon plus 2 tea-
    spoons chopped fresh
    flat-leaf parsley
Salt and freshly ground
    black pepper
¼ cup plus 1 tablespoon
    fruity olive oil

until the artichoke hearts are coarsely chopped. Add the egg yolks, lemon juice, olives, capers, parsley, and salt and pepper, and process until just blended. With the motor running, add the oil in a slow stream, until the sauce emulsifies. Let it sit, covered, for at least 1 hour, to allow the flavors to meld, then serve with the shad.

soft-shell crabs

If you've ever eaten whole blue crabs, cracking the shells with a mallet, getting crab juice all over yourself and your dinner companions, and extracting what seems like a minuscule amount of meat for your efforts, soft-shell crabs will seem like a gift from heaven: once cleaned, every last succulent bit of them is edible.

Soft-shell crabs are not a separate species but rather, hard-shell crabs caught after they have shed their old shells and before they have grown new, larger ones. Their season runs from mid-May to mid-September, with crabs from southern waters arriving as early as late March. I've been enjoying soft-shell crabs for about twenty years now and was curious as to why, in recent years, their season seems to have gotten longer. I fretted about global warming, but according to my fishmonger, it's artificial warming that accounts for the extended season: the crabs are kept near the docks in pens with warmed water, which encourages molting.

Soft-shell crabs are sweet-tasting and are delicious sautéed, deep-fried, grilled, or broiled. They go well with parsley, chervil, chives, tarragon, cilantro, ginger, and garlic. I think avocados, tomatoes, and corn are the perfect accompaniments, though I wouldn't scoff at some spinach, asparagus, or coleslaw.

Buying Criteria Some markets sell soft-shell crabs with shells that have already begun to harden; the only way to tell is to ask the fishmonger to let you touch one. Like other shellfish, soft-shell crabs should be sold alive and kicking; ask your market to kill and clean them for you and buy them the same day that you plan to cook them. If they are being sold already cleaned, take your business elsewhere: shellfish deteriorate rapidly once dead and are risky to eat if not purchased while still alive. Soft-shell crabs come in various sizes, ranging from "mediums" (3 to 3½ inches) to "whales" (over 5 inches), with "primes" (4 to 4½ inches) being the most common. Generally, a market will carry only one size on a given day, and a portion can consist of one to four crabs.

To Prepare for Cooking Most markets will clean soft-shell crabs for you, but you can easily do it yourself: wearing rubber gloves for protection, turn the crab onto its back and remove the apron (tail). Lifting up the pointed sides of the body, cut out the gills (the feathery portions) with scissors. Cut off the face and remove the sac behind it.

Soft-Shell Crabs Louis

4 servings

I've always loved crab Louis, combining, as it does, three of my favorite foods—crabs, avocados, and tomatoes—and evoking my beloved San Francisco. It also makes me think of my late aunt, Dorothy Benson, a zillionth-generation Californian who faithfully and lovingly prepared shrimp Louis for me whenever I visited her and my uncle Jimmy at their home in Walnut Creek. The traditional version uses Dungeness crabs and usually has green peppers in the sauce, with black olives scattered around; this is my version—kind of an East Coast tribute to a California classic—and to Dorothy.

Preheat an outdoor or stovetop grill, or a ridged cast-iron grill pan.

4 large soft-shell crabs, cleaned and dried well
Olive oil
Salt and freshly ground black pepper

Louis Sauce
½ cup mayonnaise
1 tablespoon heavy cream
2 tablespoons bottled chili sauce
1 tablespoon fresh lemon juice
1 tablespoon finely chopped scallion

Lightly brush the crabs with a little olive oil and season with the salt and pepper. Grill, starting shell-side down and turning once, for 7 minutes, until the flesh is opaque and the crabs feel springy, not soft, to the touch. Refrigerate or let cool to room temperature.

Make the sauce by whisking together the mayonnaise, cream, chili sauce, and lemon juice until smooth. Stir in the

2 teaspoons chopped fresh
parsley
¼ teaspoon Worcestershire
sauce
Salt and freshly ground
black pepper

4 cups mixed lettuces,
such as watercress, red
oakleaf, and Bibb
1 ripe Hass avocado,
peeled and sliced
20 cherry tomatoes, halved
4 hard-boiled eggs, cut into
wedges
1 Kirby cucumber, cut into
small dice
¼ cup diced yellow pepper

scallion, parsley, Worcestershire sauce, and salt and pepper to taste.

To serve, line four plates with lettuce, put a crab in the center, and arrange the avocado, tomatoes, and eggs around the crabs. Drizzle with the Louis Sauce and scatter the cucumber and pepper dice over all.

Soft-Shell Crabs with Asian Lime Sauce

4 servings

I love this combination of crackly-crisp crab and tart-sweet lime sauce. The sauce goes well with shrimp too.

To make the sauce, remove the peel and pith from the limes with a small sharp knife and discard. Cut the pulp into eighths. Put the lime pulp, along with all the remaining sauce ingredients except the scallion, in a food processor. Process, scraping the sides down once or twice, for 20 seconds, until the solids are broken up into small pieces. Push the sauce through a medium sieve into a bowl, pressing hard on the solids. Stir in the scallion. Cover and let stand at room temperature for 1 hour to allow the flavors to develop.

Preheat the oven to 150° F.

To cook the crabs, heat the butter and oil in a large skillet over medium heat. Lightly coat four of the crabs with cornstarch. When the fat is hot, add the crabs, season with the salt and pepper, and cook for 7 minutes, turning once,

Asian Lime Sauce
- 2 medium juicy limes
- ⅓ cup chopped fresh cilantro
- ½ teaspoon chopped garlic
- 3 tablespoons sugar
- 2 tablespoons bottled Asian fish sauce (*nam pla* or *nuoc mam*)
- 2 tablespoons water
- 1 tablespoon rice-wine vinegar
- ¼ teaspoon red pepper flakes, crumbled
- Rounded half-teaspoon finely chopped scallion, white and light green parts only

2 tablespoons unsalted butter

2 teaspoons safflower oil

8 large soft-shell crabs

Cornstarch for dredging

Salt and freshly ground black pepper

until golden and firm to the touch. Transfer to a baking sheet and keep warm in the oven. Repeat with the remaining crabs, adding more butter and oil if needed. Before serving, drain the crabs on paper towels.

Serve the crabs with individual bowls of sauce for dipping.

Soft-Shell Crabs for Pam and Judith

4 servings

In May 1991 I met with Pam Krauss, my soon-to-be editor, and my agent, Judith Weber, at a midtown Manhattan restaurant to discuss the possibility of my writing this book. When the waiter reeled off the list of specials, all three of us chose the same dish: soft-shell crabs with fresh tomatoes and herbs. It seemed the perfect thing for such a lovely spring day. The recipe below is a kind of improvisation on that dish, using the same light flavors that go so well with soft-shell crab. If you feel like grilling the crabs instead of sautéeing them, go ahead; they're great either way.

To make the Roasted Plum Tomatoes, toss the tomatoes with the olive oil and salt and pepper and place skin-side up on a broiler pan. Broil close to the heat without turning for 5 minutes, until flecked with brown. Remove from the broiler, gently toss with the vinegar, and set aside.

Roasted Plum Tomatoes
2 cups quartered ripe plum tomatoes
1 tablespoon fruity olive oil
Salt and freshly ground black pepper
½ teaspoon sherry vinegar

Preheat the oven to 150° F.

To cook the crabs, heat the butter and oil in a large skillet over medium heat. Lightly coat four of the crabs with the flour. When the fat is hot, add the crabs, season with the salt and pepper, and cook, turning once, for 7 minutes, until golden and firm to the touch. Transfer to a baking sheet and keep warm in the oven. Repeat with the remaining crabs, adding more butter and oil if needed.

Mix together the parsley, chives, and basil.

To serve, put the crabs on plates with some arugula alongside. Put the roasted tomatoes on the arugula and sprinkle them with the herbs.

2 tablespoons unsalted butter
2 teaspoons olive oil
8 large soft-shell crabs
Flour for dredging
Salt and freshly ground black pepper
2 teaspoons chopped fresh flat-leaf parsley
1½ teaspoons snipped fresh chives
1½ teaspoons chopped fresh basil
3 cups arugula

l a m b

Few foods are as evocative of spring as lamb, the traditional centerpiece of many Easter dinners. Modern breeding methods have made it possible for us to enjoy "spring" lamb all year long. However, baby or hothouse lamb, beloved by the French, Greeks, and Italians, is available at ethnic and specialty butchers almost exclusively in the spring.

American spring lamb are usually four to seven months old and about fifty pounds at slaughter. Most of our lamb comes from large ranches in Texas, California, and Colorado, where it is pasture-raised, meaning that the lambs spend most of their time outdoors and feed on grass and milk, and are usually "finished" on hay and grain. Smaller breeders sell barn-raised lamb, which are fed milk, hay, and grain and spend most of their time in the barn and barnyard. While the idea of lambs running free in hilly green pastures sounds more appealing than a herd of them kept in confinement, barn-raised lamb, according to those who raise it, is superior in flavor and texture to the pasture-raised type. Because the lambs are kept indoors, they are not subject to parasites and thus are not given drugs. And, because they are kept in a light-controlled environment that is heated in the winter and cooled in the summer, they grow faster and thus reach slaughter weight at a younger age, resulting in lighter-colored, more tender meat. Don't, however, confuse this method with the way veal calves are raised: the lambs, unlike veal calves, are in big pens in which they have room to move about freely. I've spoken to chefs and butchers about the relative merits of these two methods of raising lamb, and the consensus is that the key to tender, flavorful lamb is size, with smaller being better.

New Zealand Spring Lamb, sold frozen or defrosted in many supermarkets here, is grass-fed and usually slaughtered when it is between four and five months old. It is thus younger and smaller than most American lamb sold in supermarkets.

Baby or hothouse lamb is raised exclusively on milk, either its mother's or milk powder, and is usually between six and eight weeks old and seventeen to nineteen pounds at slaughter. Baby lamb is usually sold whole, and its meat is very pale and meltingly tender.

Lamb tastes particularly good with garlic, thyme, fennel, rosemary, herbes de Provence, mint, orange zest, black olives, and Dijon mustard—in general, any kind of Mediterranean flavoring.

Buying Criteria Because lamb is expensive, I want to make sure that I get the best quality for my money, so I prefer to buy prime lamb at a good butcher shop. If I must buy supermarket lamb and there is a choice, I find New Zealand Spring Lamb to be more reliable than the kind packaged by the store.

Choose well-trimmed lamb with off-white fat and meat whose color is slightly darker than pork but lighter than beef. A dark color is an indication of age—and consequently, of toughness and a gamy flavor.

To Prepare for Cooking If it hasn't already been done for you by the butcher, remove the fell (the hard outside layer of fat), which will give an unpleasant odor and taste to the meat. Lamb chops and roasting cuts should come to room temperature before being cooked; they will cook more evenly and quickly that way.

Lamb Sausage Patties and Marinated Vegetables on Herbed Focaccia

4 servings

This recipe, with its felicitous combination of Mediterranean flavors, was a big hit with my tasters. Don't let its length daunt you: If you're pressed for time, you can buy freshly baked focaccia at many Italian bakeries and specialty food stores.

To make the focaccia, in a small bowl stir together the water, ¼ cup plus 1 tablespoon oil, salt, and sugar. Add the yeast and stir to combine. Let sit for 5 minutes or so, until the yeast becomes foamy.

Put about 2½ cups of the flour into a large bowl, make a well in the center, and pour the yeast mixture into the well. With a wooden spoon, begin incorporating the flour into the yeast mixture, adding more flour as needed, until you have a soft, moist dough.

You can now knead the dough by hand or with an electric stand mixer with a dough hook at medium-slow speed. To knead by hand, lightly flour a countertop or wooden board, and knead for about 7 minutes, pushing the dough with the heels of your hands and then pulling it

Herbed Focaccia

1 cup warm water

¼ cup plus 1 tablespoon fruity olive oil, plus additional for the bowl and pan, and 2 tablespoons for the dough

2 teaspoons salt

2 teaspoons sugar

1 package active dry yeast

3 cups all-purpose flour (approximately)

1 tablespoon chopped fresh thyme

1¼ cups roasted red peppers, julienned

1½ teaspoons chopped fresh flat-leaf parsley

2 teaspoons fruity olive oil

1 teaspoon balsamic vinegar

3 Roasted Red Onions (page 57)

toward you with your fingers, until the dough becomes smooth, elastic, and somewhat shiny. Test to see if it is ready for rising by placing the heel of your hand on it for a few seconds; if the dough sticks, add a little more flour and knead for a few minutes longer until your hand comes away clean.

Form the dough into a ball and put it in a large, clean, lightly oiled bowl, turning the dough to coat it on all sides with the oil. Cover the bowl with plastic wrap and set it in a warm place to rise for 45 minutes, until doubled in bulk. To test the dough to see if it has risen sufficiently, press a spot with your finger; if the imprint remains, the dough is ready.

Punch the dough down with your fist, let it rest, covered, for 10 minutes, then put it into a well-oiled 9 × 12-inch baking pan, stretching it with your hands until it fills the pan in an even layer. Sprinkle the thyme over the top and press lightly so it adheres. Cover with plastic wrap and let it rise again; this rise will take only 20 minutes or so.

Preheat the oven to 400° F.

When the dough is ready, it will feel very soft all the way through and will have doubled in height. Drizzle the dough with about 2 tablespoons of olive oil and gently poke it with your fingers to make dimples. Bake for 25 minutes, or until golden. Immediately transfer

Lamb Sausage Patties

14 ounces boneless lamb
  shoulder, trimmed of fat
  and cut into 2-inch cubes
10 ounces boneless Boston
  butt (pork shoulder), cut
  into 2-inch cubes
2 tablespoons chopped
  fresh flat-leaf parsley
2 teaspoons finely chopped
  fresh rosemary
½ teaspoon minced garlic
¾ teaspoon salt
Freshly ground black pepper

the focaccia from the pan to a cooling rack, using a long spatula.

Toss the roasted red peppers with the parsley, oil, and vinegar, and set aside.

Make the Roasted Red Onions and set aside.

Place the lamb and pork in the freezer for 10 minutes, then combine in a mixing bowl. Put half of the meat mixture into the work bowl of a food processor and pulse about twenty times, until coarsely ground. Repeat with the remaining meat. Return the meat to the mixing bowl and stir in the remaining ingredients. Form into four 4-inch-diameter patties. Lightly oil a heavy skillet, get it very hot, and sear the patties over medium-high heat. Reduce the heat to medium-low and cook 10 minutes longer for medium.

To serve, cut the focaccia into 4½- or 5-inch squares and halve horizontally. Place a portion of the onions on the bottom half, top with a lamb patty, then some of the peppers, and cover with the top half of focaccia.

Provençal Roast Lamb with Olive Paste and Thyme

10 servings

My good friend and fellow chef Bob Hoebee, who visits Provence as often as possible, introduced me to this dish several years ago. It's amazingly easy to make and is wonderful for Easter dinner.

1 leg of lamb (about 6½ pounds), boned, rolled, and tied

2 or 3 garlic cloves, peeled and cut into short slivers

¼ cup Dijon mustard

¼ cup olive oil

⅓ cup olive paste (Olivada)

2 teaspoons chopped fresh thyme

½ teaspoon finely grated orange zest

Salt and freshly ground black pepper

With a sharp paring knife, make four or five dozen small shallow slits all over the lamb and push the garlic into them.

Put the remaining ingredients into a small bowl and whisk until smooth. With your hands, push some of the mixture into the folds of the roast. Rub the remainder all over the lamb. Cover and let sit at room temperature for 2 hours, or overnight in the refrigerator.

Preheat the oven to 450° F.

Place the lamb, fat-side up, in a roasting pan and roast for 10 minutes. Reduce the heat to 350° and cook the lamb about 2 hours longer for rare meat (125°–130° on an instant-read thermometer), 2½ hours for medium-rare (135°–140°). Let it rest for 15 minutes before carving.

Lamb Stew with Rosemary, Orange Zest, and Olives

4 servings

I like to serve this with buttered noodles which have been tossed with a little bit of fennel seed. Artichokes, green beans, or sugar snap peas are good accompaniments. Like most stews, this improves in flavor if made a day ahead.

Heat 2 teaspoons of the oil in a medium Dutch oven or heavy pot over medium-high heat, and brown the lamb in batches, seasoning with the salt and pepper as you go. Add more oil, if needed, to keep the meat from sticking. Set aside.

Add the remaining oil to the Dutch oven and sauté the onion over low heat for 45 minutes, until soft, sweet, and golden. Add the garlic and cook for 1 minute longer. Add the wine and boil for 2 minutes. Return the lamb to the pot and add the tomatoes, bouquet garni, olives, and sugar. Bring to a boil, lower the heat, cover tightly, and simmer for about 1½ hours, until the lamb is tender.

Discard the bouquet garni. Strain the pan juices into a saucepan and cook over

4 teaspoons olive oil

2 pounds boneless lamb shoulder, trimmed of excess fat and cut into 1½-inch cubes

Salt and freshly ground black pepper

3 cups finely chopped Spanish onion

1 teaspoon minced garlic

1 cup Côtes du Rhône or Merlot wine

**1 cup drained, chopped,
canned Italian-style
tomatoes
Bouquet garni (see Note)
¼ pound Niçoise olives,
pitted
½ teaspoon sugar
1 tablespoon chopped fresh
flat-leaf parsley
½ teaspoon chopped fresh
rosemary
Fresh orange juice**

high heat for about 3 minutes, until thickened. Return the sauce to the pot, add the parsley and rosemary, and orange juice to taste, and reheat gently.

Note: To make the bouquet garni, combine the following in a cheesecloth bag and tie the bag closed with string: One strip orange zest ($\frac{3}{4} \times 1$ inch), 1 rosemary sprig, 2 thyme sprigs, and 4 parsley stems.

spring *vegetables*

Despite my affection for cold-weather vegetables like squash, celery root, parsnips, and such, by the time spring comes, I'm filled with happy anticipation of eating artichokes, asparagus, tiny new potatoes, lush morels, fresh green peas, and sassy ramps.

Most of the vegetable dishes I cook in the spring are quick to make, leaving me more time to enjoy the balmy weather and the sight of everything green and blooming. All are intended to heighten the various flavors and textures of spring vegetables and taste rich and savory without being heavy.

a r t i c h o k e s

Although recent innovations in growing methods have made it possible for us to enjoy artichokes all year long, their peak season is from March through May, with a second mini-season in October. All of the artichokes sold in this country come from California, 75 percent from Castroville, the self-dubbed "Artichoke Capital of the World," located two hours south of San Francisco in Monterey County. I visited Castroville many years ago, before the specialty produce boom and was amazed and delighted to see the assorted shapes and sizes of one of my favorite vegetables displayed in an open-air market. I remember paying one dollar for a gigantic bag of the tiniest ones to bring back to my father in Ohio.

Baby artichokes are now available in fancy food stores across the country and are often found in supermarkets, as well. They are a blessing for cooks because they have no choke and need only to have the stem and a few tough leaves removed. Baby artichokes grow on the same plants as the large ones but closer to the ground, in the shade of the plant's fronds, where they are shielded from the sun's toughening rays. Baby artichokes can be as small as walnuts or as large as jumbo eggs. I like to marinate cooked ones in olive oil with garlic and fresh herbs, or use raw baby artichokes sliced thin in a salad with some Parmesan shavings and black olives.

The more readily available large artichokes come in two sizes: medium, which weigh 8 to 10 ounces, and large, which weigh 15 to 20 ounces. Artichokes go particularly well with seafood, veal, and pork. Compatible herbs include garlic, mint, parsley, basil, thyme, sage, and marjoram.

Buying Criteria A good artichoke will feel heavy for its size and will have a nice green color and tightly packed leaves that feel crisp and firm. In fall and winter artichokes may have bronze leaf tips or look whitish due to frost; this is fine—in fact, many people feel that the frost-kissed artichokes have the best flavor.

To Prepare for Cooking Have ready a bowl of cold water into which you've squeezed a lemon. Putting the trimmed artichokes into this will keep them from discoloring. (They will still discolor a bit, but not quite as much as without the acidulated water.) Save the cut lemon and rub each leaf with it as you go along. Bend back and snap off the tough outer leaves until you reach the central core of light green petals (the edible parts will remain attached to the base). Lop off the light green petals near their bottoms, or level with the line of broken-off leaves. Cut off the stem at the point where it meets the base of the artichoke. With a sharp knife, trim away the layer of dark green that remains on the leaves, until you expose the whitish underlayer. Remove the choke (the fuzzy center). I find it easiest to cut the artichoke in half lengthwise or even quarter it first and then use a small sharp knife, a spoon, or a combination of the two to remove the choke. This will leave you with an artichoke heart, or bottom, which is tender and completely edible.

If you want to prepare a whole artichoke for cooking or stuffing, cut off the stem, pull off the bottom row of small leaves, and remove the top quarter section of each leaf with scissors. Steam until tender, then spread apart the leaves and pull out the pale inner core of leaves. With a spoon or small knife, remove the choke.

Orecchiette with Artichokes, Sausage, and Ricotta

4 servings

My friend and colleague Kelly Kochendorfer, who was a willing guinea pig for many of the recipes in this book, declared this dish her favorite. I love it, too, with its combination of creamy, salty, and sweet flavors. For a variation try substituting peas for the artichokes.

In an 8-inch nonstick skillet, heat 1 tablespoon of the butter. Remove the sausage from its casing, crumble into olive-size pieces, and cook over medium heat, stirring often, for 5 minutes, until lightly browned. Drain on paper towels and wipe out the inside of the skillet.

Melt the remaining butter in the skillet and add the leek and carrot with salt and pepper to taste. Cover and cook over low heat for 7 minutes, until tender, stirring once or twice. Return the sausage to the skillet and add the artichokes, marjoram, and parsley. Stir to combine.

Meanwhile, cook the orecchiette in a large pot of rapidly boiling salted water,

3 tablespoons unsalted butter

½ pound sweet Italian sausage, preferably luganega

1 cup chopped leek

6 tablespoons finely diced carrot

Salt and freshly ground black pepper

2 Oven-Braised Artichokes (page 49)

**2½ teaspoons chopped
fresh marjoram**
**4 teaspoons chopped fresh
flat-leaf parsley**
2½ cups orecchiette pasta
1 cup ricotta
½ cup grated Parmesan

adding the salt right before the pasta, until al dente. Drain well and add to the skillet along with the ricotta and additional salt and pepper, if needed. Cook, tossing, over low heat, until warmed through. Stir in the Parmesan and serve immediately.

Artichoke, Pepper, and Olive Salad
with Goat Cheese Croutons

4 servings

This recipe has many variations: Try it with some cooked potatoes mixed in and omit the croutons, add the artichoke-pepper-olive mixture to pasta and serve at room temperature, or simply serve the vegetables with some shaved Parmesan on top.

To make the Green Sauce, put the walnuts in the work bowl of a food processor and process until finely chopped. Add the remaining sauce ingredients, except the oil, and process to a coarse purée. With the motor running, add the oil in a slow stream until blended. Let sit for 1 hour.

Preheat the oven to 400° F.

To make the Oven-Braised Artichokes, combine the artichokes with enough oil to cover, the garlic, thyme, and salt and pepper in a baking dish just large enough to hold them, packing them close together. Cover with foil and bake for 25 minutes, until the artichokes and garlic are tender. Discard the oil and thyme, but reserve the garlic.

Green Sauce
1½ tablespoons chopped
   walnuts
½ teaspoon chopped
   garlic
1½ teaspoons nonpareil
   capers
2 tablespoons chopped
   fresh flat-leaf parsley
¼ teaspoon finely grated
   lemon zest
1 teaspoon Dijon mustard
1 tablespoon sherry
   vinegar
Salt and freshly ground
   black pepper
¼ cup fruity olive oil

Cut the roasted peppers into ¼-inch-wide strips.

Combine the artichokes, peppers, and olives in a bowl and add enough of the Green Sauce to coat.

To make the Goat Cheese Croutons, brush the bread slices on both sides with a little olive oil and place on a baking sheet. Preheat the oven to 425° F. In a small bowl, lightly mash the goat cheese with the thyme, salt and pepper, and the reserved braised garlic. Top each bread slice with about 2 teaspoons of the mixture, mounding the cheese slightly. Bake for 10 minutes, or until the bread is golden.

To serve, arrange some mixed greens on each plate, top with a portion of the artichoke mixture in the center, and place 2 croutons on the side of each serving.

Oven-Braised Artichokes
4 large artichokes, trimmed to hearts, sliced into medium-thin wedges
Fruity olive oil
4 garlic cloves, halved
2 thyme sprigs
Salt and freshly ground black pepper

1 cup (about 1 pound) red and/or yellow bell peppers, roasted, peeled, and seeded
6 tablespoons Niçoise olives

Goat Cheese Croutons
8 ⅜-inch diagonal slices good Italian or French bread (from a long loaf about 1½ inches in diameter)
Olive oil
4 ounces soft, fresh goat cheese, such as Montrachet, at room temperature
½ teaspoon finely chopped fresh thyme
Salt and freshly ground black pepper

4 cups mixed salad greens

Veal Stew with Artichokes and Prosciutto

4 servings

Serve this with noodles, tubettini, or orzo tossed with a little olive oil or butter and grated Parmesan.

Heat 1 teaspoon of the oil in a 3-quart Dutch oven or heavy saucepan. Add the prosciutto and cook over medium heat for 2 minutes, until it starts to crisp. Remove with a slotted spoon and drain on paper towels.

In the same pan, over medium heat, heat the remaining oil and brown the veal in batches, seasoning with the salt and pepper as you go. Set aside.

2 teaspoons olive oil
4 ounces prosciutto, cut slightly thicker than usual, coarsely chopped
2 pounds boneless veal shoulder, trimmed of fat, cut into 1½-inch cubes
Salt and freshly ground black pepper
1 tablespoon unsalted butter
2 cups chopped leeks
¾ teaspoon minced garlic
½ cup dry white wine
2½ teaspoons chopped fresh sage

Add the butter to the pan, reduce the heat to low, and add the leeks with salt to taste. Cook, covered, for 10 minutes, then uncover and cook 10 minutes longer, until soft and sweet, stirring occasionally. Add the garlic and cook for 1 minute longer. Add the wine and boil for 1 minute, scraping the bottom of the pan to deglaze. Return the veal and half the prosciutto to the pan, and add the sage, tomatoes, and veal stock. Bring to a

**¾ cup seeded, chopped,
canned tomatoes**
**¼ cup veal stock (available
frozen) or chicken stock**
**2 large artichokes, trimmed
to hearts, cut into
sixteenths**

Gremolata
½ teaspoon minced garlic
**2 teaspoons chopped fresh
flat-leaf parsley**
**½ teaspoon chopped fresh
sage**
**¼ teaspoon finely grated
lemon zest**

boil over high heat, reduce the heat to low, and cook, covered, for 1 hour, until the veal is tender, adding the artichokes after 15 minutes.

In a small bowl, combine the gremolata ingredients.

Remove the veal and artichoke wedges with a slotted spoon and bring the pan liquid to a boil over high heat. Cook for 2 minutes, until the flavor intensifies and the sauce thickens slightly. Return the veal and artichoke wedges to the pan and stir in the gremolata.

Serve with a sprinkling of the reserved prosciutto on top.

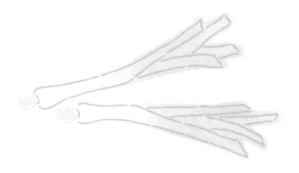

a s p a r a g u s

Like leeks, ramps, onions, and garlic, asparagus is a member of the lily family and, like lilies and other flowers, asparagus spears need to have their stem bottoms kept wet, either in water or wrapped in a damp paper towel. The California asparagus season runs from late March or early April through May, while in other, cooler, areas of the country, it runs from May through July. Asparagus range in size from pencil-thin (5/16 inch) to colossal (1 inch or more in diameter). Pencil asparagus look pretty on a plate, but I find the larger sizes to be juicier and more flavorful.

White asparagus, like Belgian endive, is covered with earth to shield it from the sun, inhibiting the production of chlorophyll, which gives vegetables their green color. Prized in Europe, white asparagus is now being grown here, but it often has a bitter edge and is very fibrous, so it must be peeled before cooking.

Buying Criteria When buying asparagus, try to find a retailer who stores it upright in about an inch of water—though I feel compelled to add that few merchants take that kind of care with asparagus. Look for asparagus with moist stem bottoms, tightly closed tips with a purplish tinge, and firm, tight skin without blemishes or wrinkles. For even cooking, choose spears that are all about the same diameter. White asparagus should be pure white, not purplish or greenish, which indicate bitterness.

To Prepare for Cooking Holding an asparagus spear at both ends, gently bend the spear; it will snap off at the point where it becomes woody. Discard the woody part, and even off the bottom with a knife. If you're serving whole asparagus spears, they will be more tender and succulent if you peel the stalks to within 2 or 3 inches of the tip with an asparagus peeler, vegetable peeler, or paring knife. Cutting asparagus on the diagonal is an alternative to peeling, because it exposes more of the tender parts. Some people like to cook asparagus in special asparagus steamers, or tie a bunch together with string and steam them upright; I've never found either method necessary. For whole spears, I bring a skillet of salted water to a simmer, lay the spears flat in it, cover, and cook until done—just a few minutes. For cut-up spears, simply bring a medium saucepan of salted water to a rapid boil, throw in the asparagus, and cook until done.

Cold Asparagus with
Watercress-Orange Mayonnaise

8 servings

I like to serve this as a first course or as an accompaniment to grilled chicken or fish. Try substituting the sauce for plain mayonnaise in potato salad.

Put the watercress, scallion, and parsley in the work bowl of a food processor and process for a few seconds, until chopped. Add the egg yolk, mustard, lemon juice, orange juice, zest, and salt and pepper, and process a few seconds longer, until blended. With the motor running, add the oil in a slow stream until the sauce has emulsified.

Transfer the sauce to a bowl, cover, and chill for 1 hour or longer to blend the flavors. The sauce can be made a day in advance and kept refrigerated.

In a skillet, cook the asparagus in boiling salted water to cover for 2-3 min-

Sauce
½ cup watercress leaves, stems discarded
1 tablespoon sliced scallion
¼ cup chopped fresh flat-leaf parsley
1 large egg yolk
1 teaspoon Dijon mustard
2 teaspoons fresh lemon juice
1 teaspoon fresh orange juice
⅛ teaspoon finely grated orange zest
Salt and freshly ground black pepper
¼ cup plus 2 tablespoons safflower oil

40 to 48 asparagus spears, trimmed and peeled

utes (covered), just until crisp-tender. Watch carefully; peeled asparagus cooks quickly. Refresh with cold water until the asparagus is cold, and dry well.

Serve the asparagus napped with the sauce.

Asparagus and Red Onion Tart

4 to 6 servings

This is a variation on a tart that my friend Bob Hoebee often makes. Its pretty pastel shades look very springlike.

To make the Pâte Brisée, combine the flour, butter, salt, and sugar in a food processor and pulse about eight times, until the butter pieces are the size of large peas. Add 2 tablespoons of the water, sprinkling it over the flour mixture, and process for 3 seconds.

Transfer to a lightly floured surface. If the dough seems dry, add a little more water. Toss the mixture with your hands to incorporate the water, then blend by pushing the dough down and away from you with the heels of your hands, working in sections. Form into a thick disk, cover with plastic wrap, and refrigerate for at least 1 hour.

Pâte Brisée
1 cup flour
7 tablespoons frozen butter, cut into 28 pieces
½ teaspoon salt
⅛ teaspoon sugar
2 to 3 tablespoons ice water, approximately

Before rolling, let the dough sit for 5 minutes, then roll it out into a 12-inch circle and fit it into a 9-inch pie or tart pan. Prick all over with a fork, cover, and chill for 1 hour.

Meanwhile, make the Roasted Red Onions. Preheat the oven to 450° F. Cut the onions crosswise into ⅜-inch-thick slices. Spread half the oil in a 9-inch square baking pan, add the onions in a single layer, and drizzle the remaining oil over

Roasted Red Onions

2 small red onions (about 3
    ounces each), peeled,
    both ends trimmed
2 tablespoons olive oil
2 thyme sprigs
Salt and freshly ground
    black pepper

Filling

10 asparagus spears,
    trimmed, cut into 1½-inch
    diagonal pieces
3 large egg yolks
1 cup heavy cream
2 teaspoons chopped fresh
    tarragon
Salt and freshly ground
    black pepper
⅓ cup coarsely grated
    Emmenthal, fontina, or
    Gruyère cheese
1 teaspoon unsalted butter

them. Break up the thyme sprigs and put a piece on each onion slice. Season with the salt and pepper, cover with foil, and bake for 20 minutes. Uncover and bake 5 minutes longer, until the bottoms become golden. Discard the thyme. Lower the oven temperature to 375° F.

Weigh the dough down with pie weights or beans set into foil. Bake for 10 minutes, then remove the weights and foil and bake for 3 minutes longer, until the shell is just beginning to color. Do not turn off the oven.

Cook the asparagus until crisp-tender in a pot of rapidly boiling salted water. Refresh with cold water until thoroughly cool, then dry well with paper towels.

In a bowl, gently whisk the egg yolks, cream, tarragon, and salt and pepper until blended.

Arrange the onions and asparagus attractively in the pie shell, pour the custard over, and sprinkle with the cheese. Dot the tart with the butter, place on a baking sheet, and bake in the upper third of the oven for 25 to 30 minutes, until the custard is puffy.

Serve warm or at room temperature.

fiddlehead ferns

Fiddlehead ferns, so named because they resemble the carved scrolls of a fiddle, are not a specific variety of fern but rather the coiled fronds of young edible ferns (usually ostrich or weed ferns) that have just emerged from the soil. Fiddleheads grow along rivers and streams on the East Coast as far north as Newfoundland, south to Virginia, and west to the midsection of the country, and are most abundant in Maine. The season for wood ferns runs from March to May, and ostrich ferns are harvested from June to July.

Fiddleheads have a fresh, verdant flavor similar to green beans, but with hints of asparagus and artichokes, and may be cooked just as you would any of those kindred vegetables.

Buying Criteria Select small (less than 1½ inches in diameter), firm, tightly curled fiddleheads with little or no tail. They should be bright green under their brown papery skin. Since fiddleheads quickly lose their fresh taste, it's best to use them within a day of purchasing.

To Prepare for Cooking Rub off the skin, trim the tails close to the curled base, and rinse with cold water.

Fiddlehead, Yellow Pepper, and Tomato Salad with Mustardy Dressing

8 servings

1 pound fiddlehead ferns, trimmed

1 yellow pepper (about ½ pound), cut into ¼-inch-wide strips

4 medium plum tomatoes, seeded, cut into ¼-inch-wide strips

2 tablespoons plus 2 teaspoons finely chopped red onion

1 tablespoon plus 1 teaspoon chopped fresh flat-leaf parsley

¼ cup chopped fresh basil

¼ cup Dijon mustard

2 tablespoons balsamic vinegar

2 tablespoons fruity olive oil

Salt and freshly ground black pepper

Cook the fiddleheads in rapidly boiling salted water to cover for 1 or 2 minutes, until crisp-tender. Refresh under cold running water until thoroughly cool, and dry well with paper towels. Combine in a bowl with the pepper, tomatoes, onion, parsley, and basil.

In a small bowl, whisk the mustard and vinegar until blended. Add the oil in a slow stream, whisking constantly, until emulsified.

Pour the dressing over the vegetables, season with the salt and pepper, and toss well to blend.

Sautéed Fiddleheads and Eggs
on Challah Toast

1 serving

With a nice salad and a glass of wine, this makes a lovely spring lunch or light supper. Depending on your mood and the contents of your refrigerator, you can try this with asparagus or ramps instead of fiddleheads, and use chervil or parsley instead of chives. If you're so inclined, add a little grated cheese, such as Parmesan, fontina, or Gruyère. I happen to prefer it without cheese so that the clear, pure flavors of the fiddleheads and chives can shine.

In an 8-inch nonstick skillet, warm the butter and oil over medium heat. When the foam subsides, add the fiddleheads and salt and pepper, and cook, tossing often, for 2 minutes, until crisp-tender. With a slotted spoon, transfer to a plate and cover loosely with foil to keep warm.

Reduce the heat to low and add the eggs, seasoned with salt and pepper. Scramble to your liking.

Divide the eggs among the two pieces of toast, top with the fiddleheads, and sprinkle with the snipped chives. Serve immediately.

2 teaspoons unsalted butter
1 teaspoon olive oil
¼ pound fiddlehead ferns, trimmed
Salt and freshly ground black pepper
3 large eggs, beaten
2 slices challah or brioche, toasted
1½ teaspoons snipped fresh chives

Pappardelle with Fiddleheads and Shrimp

4 servings

Bring a large pot of water to a rolling boil for the pasta.

Combine the butter with the oil in a large nonstick skillet. Heat to foaming over medium heat and add the fiddleheads. Cook, tossing frequently and seasoning with salt and pepper, for 3 minutes, until almost crisp-tender. Remove the fiddleheads with a slotted spoon and transfer to a plate. Add the tomato to the skillet and cook for 1 minute, then remove with a slotted spoon and add to the fiddleheads. Cook the shrimp in the same skillet, seasoning with salt and pepper and tossing, for 2 minutes, until pink. Remove with a slotted spoon and add to the vegetables. Remove the skillet from the heat, and when it is cool, return the shrimp and vegetables to the pan; stir in the cream, saffron, parsley, and chives.

Cook the pasta according to the package directions until al dente. Drain well, then add the pasta to the skillet, turning the heat to medium-high, and cook, tossing well with two forks, for about a minute.

1 tablespoon unsalted butter
1 teaspoon olive oil
½ pound fiddlehead ferns, trimmed
Salt and freshly ground black pepper
½ cup finely diced seeded ripe plum tomato
32 medium shrimp (about ¾ pound), peeled and deveined
¾ cup heavy cream
Small pinch saffron threads
2 tablespoons chopped fresh flat-leaf parsley
2 tablespoons snipped fresh chives
¾ pound egg pappardelle

s p r i n g   g r e e n s

Spring is prime season for four kinds of greens: spinach, dandelion greens, arugula, and sorrel. When young and tender, these greens may be used raw in salads, and greens at any stage may be braised, sautéed, or made into soups.

Fresh, young spinach, bought either loose or in bunches, can be a revelatory experience, but avoid the prepackaged bags. I find that the flatter, pointed-leaf variety has a finer flavor than the more common bumpy-leafed type. The assertive flavor of raw spinach goes well with creamy or eggy salad dressings.

Eating dandelion greens that have been sautéed in olive oil with garlic and a splash of lemon will make you forget their association with those pesky weeds that proliferate on lawns. Almost all of the dandelions sold in markets are cultivated, not wild, and taste less bitter than the wild variety. Southerners, with their love of braised greens of all types, have long prized dandelion greens, as have Italians. It was, in fact, at the home of the Morettonis, Roman friends of mine who live in San Francisco, that I had my first taste of dandelions, which Marcella Morettoni called "cicoria." They can sometimes be found in supermarkets and farmers' markets, and they are a staple at stores in Italian neighborhoods. Young raw dandelions are delicious with a sweet-and-sour boiled dressing.

Peppery, mustardy arugula (also known as rocket), though mostly used raw in salads, is delicious when cooked, and because of its wider availability and similar flavor and texture, makes a good substitute for dandelions.

Sorrel, like arugula, is something most people either love or hate at first bite. The tart, lemony taste that inspired its other name, sour grass, is so distinct and particular that no one can remain neutral about it. Those of us who grew up in Jewish households are familiar with sorrel as the main ingredient in *schav*, a cold, creamy puréed soup. In France, where it is known as *oseille*, it is cooked and puréed, with cream or eggs added, and used in soups or as a tart sauce for poultry and fish (particularly shad). It can also be used raw, as an herb.

Buying Criteria When buying greens look for good green color, perky leaves, and thin stems. Remember that because of their high water content, greens shrink tremendously when cooked. In general, 2 to 3 pounds of raw greens will yield 2 cups of cooked.

To Prepare for Cooking Greens, particularly spinach and arugula, tend to be very sandy and must be cleaned carefully. Fill a bowl or the sink with cold water, put the greens in, and slosh them around for a few seconds. Give the grit a few minutes to settle to the bottom, remove the greens, change the water, and repeat until no grit remains. Trim off any thick stems and discolored or limp leaves and dry well.

Use nonreactive pans for cooking; otherwise the greens will pick up an "off" taste and will discolor.

Polenta *Torta* with
Sautéed Spring Greens and Pancetta

6 servings

This is a great dish for spring entertaining: It can be prepared up to the point of baking a day ahead of time, refrigerated, and baked before serving. (If you do this allow an additional 5 to 10 minutes' baking time.)

Cook the pancetta in a large skillet over low heat, stirring often, until golden brown, about 15 minutes. Drain on paper towels. Pour off the fat from the skillet.

Heat 2 tablespoons of the oil and the garlic in the same skillet over medium heat. Add the greens and salt and pepper, and cook, stirring, until the ribs of the greens are just tender, about 4 minutes. Discard the garlic and toss the greens in a bowl with the pancetta.

Preheat the oven to 450° F.

To make the polenta, combine the cornmeal with 1 cup of the water. Bring the remaining water to a boil in a large heavy saucepan. Reduce the heat to low and slowly stir in the cornmeal mixture

3 ounces pancetta, cut into ⅜-inch dice

2 tablespoons plus 2 teaspoons fruity olive oil

1 medium garlic clove, hit once with the flat side of a knife and peeled

6 ounces spinach, stemmed and torn into pieces

2 ounces dandelion greens, stemmed and torn into pieces

2 ounces arugula, stemmed and torn into pieces

**Salt and freshly ground
  black pepper**
1½ cups yellow cornmeal
5 cups water
**2 ounces pecorino Romano,
  grated**
**4 ounces Fontina Val
  D'Aosta, grated**

with a wire whisk. Whisk until smooth, then cook, stirring constantly with a wooden spoon, until it is thick and the bottom of the pan is visible when you stir, about 20 minutes. Stir in the pecorino Romano and add salt to taste.

Spread one-third of the polenta in a well-buttered 1½-quart round baking dish and top with half of the greens and one-third of the fontina. Make one more layer of polenta, greens, and fontina, then top with the remaining polenta and fontina. Drizzle the *torta* with the remaining 2 teaspoons of olive oil.

Place the dish on a baking sheet and bake until the *torta* is firm and beginning to brown, about 15 minutes. Cool for 5 minutes before serving in wedges.

Chicken Soup with Arugula and Little Dumplings

4 servings

I've loved the combination of bitter greens and chicken soup ever since I first tasted it years ago at an Italian restaurant. Other greens such as spinach or broccoli rabe can be used in place of arugula. For a simple and delicious pasta dish, cook the dumplings in broth or water, drain well, and toss with some butter, grated cheese and plenty of black pepper.

1 egg, beaten
1 tablespoon grated pecorino Romano
2 teaspoons finely chopped fresh flat-leaf parsley
¼ cup water
¼ teaspoon salt
Freshly ground black pepper to taste
½ cup plus 2 tablespoons flour
4 cups chicken stock, preferably homemade
5 cups chopped arugula, cut into 2-inch pieces

In a bowl mix the egg with the cheese, parsley, water, salt, and pepper. Sift the flour over the mixture and stir to blend. The mixture should be the consistency of muffin batter; if not; add flour or water accordingly. Cover the bowl with plastic wrap and let sit at room temperature for 1 hour.

Bring the chicken stock to a simmer and add the arugula. Cook for 5 minutes, until tender, then remove the greens with a slotted spoon or tongs.

With a rubber spatula, push the

dumpling batter through the holes of a slotted spoon or similar implement into the soup, about a half-cup at a time, until all the batter is used. The dumplings are done when they come to the surface, which takes just a few seconds.

Return the arugula to the pot, stir, and serve immediately.

wild mushrooms

Though wild mushrooms, with their bosky flavor, may seem more evocative of autumn, several have their peak season in the spring, with full-flavored cèpes and morels the most eminent.

cèpes

Cèpes are known as boletes in the United States and, perhaps more familiarly, by their Italian name, porcini. With their domed caps and chunky, bulbous stems, they've always reminded me of something out of *Fantasia*. Cèpes have long been prized in Europe, where they are available both fresh and dried. Although grown in the United States, with some of the best specimens coming from the northern West Coast, they are in scant supply at markets because their stems are frequently infested with little worms. Because of their scarcity, they can be frightfully expensive, usually costing between $25 and $40 a pound. However, cèpes have an unparalleled taste—meaty, robust, and earthy—which makes them well worth seeking out during their short season in May. Try them grilled whole, or sliced and sautéed in olive oil with a bit of garlic and fresh herbs. They are exquisite in a reduced cream sauce over pasta, in a risotto, or with just about any kind of meat. Dried cèpes, available in specialty stores, have an intense flavor; a little goes a long way.

Buying Criteria Choose firm cèpes with caps about 6 inches across, and check the stems for worms; if there are any, simply cut away that portion before cooking. Elizabeth Schneider, in *Uncommon Fruits and Vegetables: A Commonsense Guide*, recommends choosing those whose caps have the palest undersides.

To Prepare for Cooking Wipe clean with a mushroom brush or a damp paper towel and trim the stem bottoms.

m o r e l s

When morels begin making their appearance in the markets in late March, my heart gives a little leap, knowing that winter is over and spring is truly here. Prevalent in the Pacific Northwest and parts of the Midwest and East Coast, these harbingers of spring have a distinctive appearance: a honeycomb-textured, elongated cone-shaped cap atop a hollow stem. Like truffles, to which they are related, morels are much sought after and extravagantly priced. They have a subtle, smoky, nutty flavor that is an ideal match for light meats, starches, and grains. Their spongy caps soak up sauces beautifully. But don't be tempted to eat them raw; they may make you ill. Morels are available until mid-July.

Buying Criteria Choose morels that look neither wet nor dried-out, with an earthy, woodsy aroma. For ease of preparation, try to select ones that are as clean as possible; morel caps frequently hold a considerable amount of dirt.

To Prepare for Cooking Wipe clean with a mushroom brush or a damp paper towel and trim the stem bottoms. If the morels are very dirty, rinse them quickly under cold running water and wipe dry immediately. To show off their appealing shape, try to leave them whole or halved.

Grits with Cèpes, Mascarpone, and Sweet Garlic

4 servings

This dish was inspired by Giuliano Bugialli's recipe for polenta with mascarpone and shaved white truffles, an incredible combination of flavors but, given the price of fresh truffles, very costly. In this version, the sweet garlic contributes an earthiness of flavor evocative of fresh truffles. Serve this as a first course for a meat dinner.

To make the Sweet Garlic, place the garlic cloves in a small ramekin with oil to cover, cover with foil, and bake in a preheated 325° F. oven for 30 minutes, until completely tender. Let cool, then peel the garlic, trim off the root ends, and chop to a purée. Discard the oil. Set aside, covered.

Sweet Garlic
16 medium garlic cloves, unpeeled
Olive oil

Grits
2¾ cups chicken or veal stock
¾ cup water
Salt
¾ cup grits

To cook the grits, bring the stock and water to a rolling boil. Add the salt and grits in a slow stream, stirring constantly, until smooth. Cover and cook over low heat, stirring occasionally, for 15 to 20 minutes, until thick.

To make the cèpes, heat the butter and oil in a medium skillet and add the cèpes. Cook over medium heat, stirring often, for 10 min-

Cèpes

**1 tablespoon unsalted
butter**

2 teaspoons olive oil

**10 ounces fresh cèpes,
stems trimmed, caps cut
into ¼-inch-thick slices**

**Salt and freshly ground
black pepper**

**2 teaspoons finely chopped
fresh flat-leaf parsley**

4 tablespoons mascarpone

utes, until tender. Add the salt and pepper after the cèpes have begun to wilt. Stir in the parsley and Sweet Garlic and remove from the heat.

To serve, spoon a little mascarpone on each plate, top with the grits, and place the cèpes on top. Serve immediately.

Morel and Ramp Custard

4 servings

If you've ever eaten the delicate Japanese custard called chawan mushi, *you'll have some idea of what this dish is like. The soft, bland custard is the perfect foil for the assertive flavors of the ramps and morels. Ramps, which are wild leeks, have a very potent flavor and aroma that belie their genteel appearance. They are in season from March to June, but if you can't find them, substitute leeks or scallions in this recipe.*

Combine the cream and milk in a small saucepan and heat almost to scalding.

Remove the green tops from the ramps, reserving the bulbs, and add a 1-inch piece of green top to the milk mixture. Add the reserved morel stems and 1 thyme sprig to the milk mixture, cover the pan, and infuse for 1 hour.

Coarsely chop the ramps; you should have 2 tablespoons.

While the milk mixture infuses, heat the butter in an 8-inch skillet and add the morels and salt and pepper, plus the remaining thyme sprig. Cook over me-

¾ cup heavy cream

¾ cup milk

8 ramps, rinsed well, trimmed

¼ pound morels, stemmed and julienned, 6 stems reserved

2 small thyme sprigs

2 teaspoons unsalted butter, plus additional if needed

Salt and freshly ground black pepper

3 large eggs

1 large egg yolk
½ teaspoon kosher salt
2 teaspoons finely chopped
** fresh flat-leaf parsley**

dium heat for 7 minutes, until tender. Remove with a slotted spoon and drain on paper towels. If the skillet is dry, add a little more butter. Add the ramps, season with salt and pepper, and cook, covered, over low heat, for 5 minutes, until tender and translucent.

In a medium bowl, whisk the eggs, egg yolk, the ½ teaspoon kosher salt, and pepper to taste until just blended but not foamy. Strain the milk mixture into the eggs, whisking gently.

In another bowl, mix the morels with the ramps. Preheat the oven to 325° F.

Lightly butter four 6-ounce porcelain ramekins and divide the morel mixture evenly among them. Pour the custard mixture into the ramekins and set them into a small baking dish. Put the pan on the middle rack of the oven. With a liquid measuring cup or teapot, carefully add hot tap water to come halfway up the sides of the ramekins. Gently slide the oven rack back into place, and bake for 25 minutes, until set.

Remove the ramekins from the water and let sit 5 minutes before unmolding. (You can also serve the custards in the ramekins.) Sprinkle with the parsley before serving.

Broiled Polenta with
Sautéed Mushrooms and Leeks

4 servings

In a liquid measuring cup, combine the milk and stock. Put the cornmeal in a bowl and add ½ cup of the milk mixture; stir to blend. Bring the remaining milk mixture to a boil in a heavy-bottomed saucepan. Reduce the heat to low and slowly whisk in the cornmeal mixture, stirring constantly with a wooden spoon. Add salt and pepper to taste. Cook, stirring, for 15 to 20 minutes, until the polenta is thick and the bottom of the pan is visible as you stir.

Pour the polenta into a 9-inch round cake pan and smooth out the top with a frosting spatula or dinner knife. Let cool, then cover and refrigerate for 2 hours or overnight.

To make the Sautéed Mushrooms and Leeks, heat the oil in a 10-inch skillet and add the leeks, salt, and one thyme sprig. Cook, covered, over low heat for 10 minutes, until soft. Uncover and cook 10 minutes longer, until sweet and meltingly tender. Scrape into a bowl and add a little more oil to the pan, if needed. Add the mushrooms, salt and pepper, and the remaining thyme sprig, and

Polenta
1 cup milk
⅔ cup chicken stock
½ cup yellow cornmeal
**Salt and freshly ground
 black pepper**
2 teaspoons fruity olive oil

**Sautéed Mushrooms and
 Leeks**
**2 tablespoons fruity olive
 oil, plus additional if
 needed**
2 cups chopped leeks

Salt and freshly ground
  black pepper
2 small thyme sprigs
6 ounces shiitake mush-
  rooms, stems discarded,
  caps cut into ¼-inch-thick
  slices
4 ounces morels, stems
  discarded, caps halved
  lengthwise (or leave
  whole if small)
½ teaspoon minced garlic
2 ounces veal demi-glace
  (see Note) or chicken
  stock
1 tablespoon chopped fresh
  flat-leaf parsley
Watercress (optional)

cook over medium-low heat for 15 minutes, stirring occasionally, until almost
tender. Add the garlic and cook 1
minute longer. Stir in the demi-glace
and cook over low heat for 2 minutes,
until it is absorbed. Discard the thyme
sprigs, then stir in the chopped parsley
and reserved leeks, and keep warm.
Preheat the broiler.

Cut the polenta into six wedges and
brush on both sides with the oil. Arrange
on a well-oiled broiler pan and cook on
the lowest rack of the broiler for 5 minutes, until flecked with brown.

To serve as a first course, put a little watercress on each plate,
top with a polenta wedge, and spoon the mushroom mixture over.
To serve as a side dish, tuck a sprig of watercress alongside the
mushroom-topped polenta, if desired.

Note: Excellent frozen veal demi-glace may be mail-ordered
from D'Artagnan, 399 St. Paul Avenue, Jersey City, N.J. 07306;
800-327-8246.

Wild Mushroom Lasagna

4 servings

Use a combination of strong-flavored (such as morels, cèpes, or shi-itakes) and delicate-flavored (chanterelles, trumpets, or oysters) mushrooms in this dish.

To make the Béchamel, melt the butter over medium heat in a heavy, medium saucepan. When it foams, add the flour and cook, stirring, for 3 minutes. Stir in the warm half-and-half and cook, stirring, for a few minutes, until thickened. Add the remaining ingredients, cover, and place over a pan of simmering water. Cook, stirring occasionally, for 45 minutes. Remove the bouquet garni, and cover the pot.

While the sauce cooks, prepare the lasagna: Heat the butter and oil until foamy in a 10-inch skillet or sauté pan over medium heat. Add the mushrooms and cook for 5 minutes, until slightly wilted. Add the shallots, parsley, sage, and salt and pepper, and cook, stirring, for 6 minutes, until tender. Add the stock, raise the heat to high, and cook, stirring, for 2 minutes, until the stock is absorbed.

Cook the pasta in a large pot of rapidly boiling salted water for 3

Béchamel
2 tablespoons unsalted butter
2 tablespoons all-purpose flour
2 cups half-and-half, scalded
Salt and freshly ground black pepper
Bouquet garni (see Note)

Lasagna

1 tablespoon unsalted butter
1 tablespoon olive oil
1½ pounds assorted fresh wild mushrooms, stems discarded, caps thinly sliced
¾ cup chopped shallots
⅓ cup chopped fresh flat-leaf parsley
2 tablespoons chopped fresh sage
Salt and freshly ground black pepper
½ cup chicken stock
½ pound fresh spinach pasta sheets, cut into 3½ x 8-inch rectangles
½ cup freshly grated Parmesan
Additional butter for dotting the top

minutes, until cooked halfway. Drain in a colander, rinse with cold water, and put the pasta in a bowl or deep pan filled with cold water and a little oil. Have paper towels or a clean dish towel handy so that you can dry the pasta before layering it with the other ingredients. Preheat the oven to 450° F.

Lightly coat the bottom of an 8-inch square baking pan with some of the Béchamel. Top with a layer of pasta, cover with one-quarter of the Béchamel, and sprinkle with one-quarter of the Parmesan. Spread one third of the mushrooms evenly over the cheese. Continue making layers in this manner, ending with Béchamel and Parmesan. Scatter dots of butter over the top and place on a baking sheet.

Bake on the top rack of the oven for 10 to 15 minutes, until puffy and golden. Let the lasagna sit for 5 minutes before cutting.

Note: To make the bouquet garni, combine the following in a cheesecloth bag and tie the bag closed with string: 1 small sprig of sage, 1 small sprig of thyme, 2 stems of parsley, 2 garlic cloves, peeled and halved, and 1 small shallot, peeled and halved.

n e w   p o t a t o e s

Contrary to popular opinion, new potatoes are not the small red or white potatoes that abound in produce markets all year long but rather, freshly dug potatoes of any variety that are picked young and have never been stored. Most of the "new" potatoes that we see have actually been picked months ago and kept in storage to prolong their availability in the market.

In most parts of the country, the fresh potato crop begins in July, but some early varieties come up in warmer areas in May. That said, I must admit that I absolutely have to have "new" potatoes for Easter dinner, cut up and roasted with olive oil, garlic, and herbs, or steamed and tossed with butter and parsley. Their "newness," however illusory, evokes for me the rebirth of the earth and the promise of more good things to come.

The recipes that follow should be made with waxy, rather than mealy (Idaho-type), potatoes. The various specialty potatoes—such as Yukon Gold, yellow Finn, fingerling, creamer, and purple Peruvian—that have recently become available also work well in these recipes. Seek them out at farmers' markets and specialty stores; they are utterly delicious, some so buttery-tasting that they need only salt and pepper.

Buying Criteria Choose firm potatoes without cracks, "eyes," bruises, wrinkled skins, or a greenish tinge.

To Prepare for Cooking Scrub well in cold water with a vegetable brush. Peel or not, according to your taste and how you want the finished dish to look. Cut away any eyes, bruises, or greenish areas.

Roasted New Potatoes
with Scallions, Dill, and Cream

4 to 6 servings

Serve this with salmon and peas or sugar snaps, or with grilled chicken. It's also great with eggs for breakfast.

Preheat the oven to 450° F.

In a medium bowl, toss the potatoes with the oil and salt and pepper. Put the potatoes in an ovenproof 10-inch skillet or sauté pan and bake on the top rack of the oven for 25 to 30 minutes, until tender and lightly browned, tossing several times during cooking.

Transfer the skillet to the stovetop, add the scallion and cream, and cook over medium heat for a minute or two, scraping the bottom of the pan to get all the browned bits, until the cream is absorbed. Stir in the dill and serve immediately.

1½ pounds new potatoes, skins on, cut into ¾-inch dice

¼ cup olive oil

Salt and freshly ground black pepper

¼ cup chopped scallion, including a little of the dark green parts

3 ounces heavy cream (not the ultrapasteurized type)

1 rounded tablespoon chopped fresh dill

New Potato Salad with
Bacon, Tarragon, and Chives

4 servings

This is a good recipe to play around with. You can substitute red onion or shallots for the chives, dill or parsley for the tarragon. It tastes best when not refrigerated.

Preheat the oven to 450° F.

In a medium bowl, toss the potatoes with the oil and salt and pepper. Transfer to a 9 × 13-inch baking dish, and cook on the top rack of the oven for 25 to 30 minutes, tossing several times, until tender and lightly browned. Let cool.

Cook the bacon slowly in a skillet over low heat until crisp. Drain on paper towels.

When the potatoes and bacon have cooled, toss them in a bowl with the remaining ingredients, adding more salt and pepper if needed. Serve at room temperature.

1½ pounds new potatoes, skins on, cut into 1-inch wedges

2 tablespoons olive oil

Salt and freshly ground black pepper

¼ pound slab bacon, cut into ⅜-inch dice

4 teaspoons snipped fresh chives

4 teaspoons chopped fresh tarragon

1 tablespoon Dijon mustard

2 tablespoons mayonnaise

Coarse-Mashed New Potatoes with Dandelions and Garlic

4 servings

1¼ pounds small red new potatoes, scrubbed and halved

Salt and freshly ground black pepper

3 tablespoons fruity olive oil

3 garlic cloves, peeled, crushed lightly with the flat side of a knife

¾ pound dandelion greens, trimmed, chopped into 2-inch pieces

Put the potatoes in a medium saucepan with cold water to cover by 1 inch. Add salt and bring to a boil over high heat. Reduce the heat to low, cover, and cook for 5 minutes, until tender.

Meanwhile, cook the dandelion greens. Heat 2 tablespoons of the oil and the garlic in an 8-inch skillet over medium heat. When the garlic is fragrant, add the dandelions and salt and pepper, and cook for 3 minutes, until tender. If the garlic threatens to brown, discard it. Drain off any liquid that accumulates in the pan.

With a fork or potato masher, coarsely mash the potatoes, seasoning with salt, pepper, and the remaining oil. Fold in the dandelions and serve immediately.

p e a s   a n d   s u g a r   s n a p s

There's something so inherently appealing about peas that even avowed vegetable haters will eat them—perhaps it's their tiny size and simple, sweet flavor. As a child whose other vegetable preferences were limited to corn, potatoes, and creamed spinach, I loved going with my mother to our local greengrocer to buy peas in the pod, which I ate raw, right there in the store. To this day, shelling fresh peas and popping them into my mouth remains my favorite way of eating them, though I do love them cooked simply, as a side dish with a little ham or prosciutto tossed in, in soups and shellfish stews, and with pasta or rice.

Fresh peas are in season from April through July. Fresh petits pois, though hard to find and time-consuming to shell, are delicious and adorable.

Buying Criteria As with corn, the high sugar content that makes peas so delicious quickly turns to starch with age. It's best to buy them where they're most likely to be freshest, at a farm stand or farmers' market. Many stores sell peas already shelled, which, while convenient, gives you no way of ascertaining their freshness or flavor; avoid them. Look for small pods, which indicate younger, sweeter peas. My colleague Sally Belk contends that wrinkled pods are also indicative of sweeter peas, and she suggests rubbing two pods together; if they squeak, they're fresh.

To Prepare for Cooking Simply pull the pod apart at the seam and run your finger down its length to extricate the peas.

sugar snap peas

Introduced to the market in 1979, sugar snaps are a pea lover's dream. A cross between green peas and snow peas, sugar snaps look like garden peas, but both the pods and the peas inside are edible, and in my experience, consistently sweet-tasting. I like to prepare them very simply, with various herb butters and a squeeze of lemon, in mixed vegetable sautés, or as a sweeter alternative to snow peas in stir-fries (they're particularly good with scallops). Like peas, they go well with just about any kind of meat, fish, or poultry. Fresh local sugar snaps are available from May through August.

Buying Criteria Choose small, plump, firm, bright green sugar snaps.

To Prepare for Cooking Destring by snapping off the stem end and pulling down so that the thread detaches along the seam.

Angel Hair Pasta with Peas and Leeks

4 servings

This dish looks and tastes like spring to me, with its three shades of green from the leeks, peas, and chervil, and delicate fresh taste.

In a 10-inch skillet, heat 2 tablespoons of the butter over low heat. Add the leeks, salt and pepper, and thyme. Cover and cook for 7 minutes, until the leeks are wilted and pale green. Uncover and cook for 5 minutes longer, until the leeks are almost completely tender, with just a little crunch. Discard the thyme. Transfer the leeks to a bowl and add the peas and chervil. Taste for salt and pepper. When the leeks have cooled, return to the skillet.

Cook the pasta in a large pot of rapidly boiling salted water, adding the salt right before the pasta until al dente (3 minutes for dried pasta, 1 minute for fresh). Drain well in a colander.

Add the pasta to the skillet, along with the stock and remaining 2 tablespoons of butter, and cook over medium heat for 2 minutes, or until the stock is absorbed. Stir in the lemon juice and Parmesan.

4 tablespoons (½ stick) unsalted butter
2 cups julienned leeks
Salt and freshly ground black pepper
1 thyme sprig
1½ cups cooked green peas, as small as possible
2 tablespoons chopped fresh chervil
¾ pound dried angel hair pasta or 1 pound fresh
¾ cup chicken stock
Fresh lemon juice to taste
Freshly grated Parmesan to taste

Warm Sugar Snap Salad with Bacon, Pecans, and Cider Vinegar

2 to 3 servings

In a medium skillet over low heat, cook the bacon until crisp. Remove with a slotted spoon and drain on paper towels.

Pour off all but 2 teaspoons of fat from the skillet. Add the sugar snaps and cook over medium heat, tossing often, for 3 minutes, until crisp-tender.

In a small bowl, beat the mustard with the vinegar and salt and pepper until combined. Slowly whisk in the olive oil until blended. Add to the sugar snaps in the skillet, along with the bacon, pecans, parsley, and scallion. Toss well to warm through and serve immediately.

4 ounces slab bacon, cut into ⅜-inch dice

½ pound sugar snaps, strings removed

1½ teaspoons Dijon mustard

4 teaspoons cider vinegar

Salt and freshly ground black pepper

4 teaspoons olive oil

3 tablespoons pecans, toasted

2 teaspoons chopped fresh flat-leaf parsley

1 tablespoon chopped scallion

Chilled Pea Soup
with Buttermilk and Chervil

6 to 8 servings

Delicate and sweet, with a soft pistachio color, this makes a good first course for a chicken or salmon meal.

To make the stock, shell the peas and set aside. Combine the empty pea pods with the remaining stock ingredients in a large pot. Bring to a boil, lower the heat, and simmer for 30 minutes, stirring occasionally. Strain through a colander, pressing hard on the solids with a spoon. You will have about 6 cups of stock. Transfer to a clean pot and reduce over medium-low heat until you have 5 cups.

While the stock cooks, heat the butter in a clean pot. Add the leeks and salt, cover, and cook over low heat for 10 minutes, until the leeks have softened. Uncover and cook 15 minutes longer, until the leeks are meltingly tender.

Add the pea stock and bring to a boil. Add the reserved peas, salt, and pepper. Simmer until the peas are tender; this will vary from 5 to 10 minutes, depend-

Pea Stock
3 pounds fresh peas
8 Boston lettuce leaves
**1 cup watercress leaves
and stems**
**¾ cup coarsely chopped
scallion, including the
green tops**
**1 cup coarsely chopped
celery and leaves**
6 chervil sprigs
8 cups water
Salt
**2 teaspoons sugar (optional,
depending on the sweet-
ness of the peas)**

**1 tablespoon unsalted
   butter
2 cups chopped leeks
Salt
3 cups peas, approximately,
   reserved from Pea Stock
Freshly ground black
   pepper
1 cup buttermilk
2 tablespoons chopped
   fresh chervil
Chervil leaves for garnish**

ing on size and freshness. Let the soup cool slightly.

Purée the soup in a blender, then strain through a sieve, pressing hard on the solids with a spoon. Stir in the buttermilk and chervil and refrigerate, covered, until cold.

Garnish each serving with a few chervil leaves.

Sautéed Sugar Snaps
with Chives and Lemon

2 to 3 servings

I love this dish—it's fast and easy to prepare and goes with just about any meat, fish, or poultry entree. The tang of fresh lemon is a nice counterpoint to the sweet sugar snaps.

1½ tablespoons unsalted butter
½ pound sugar snaps
Salt and freshly ground black pepper
4 teaspoons snipped fresh chives
Fresh lemon juice to taste

Heat the butter until foamy in an 8-inch nonstick skillet over medium heat. Add the sugar snaps and salt and pepper and cook, tossing often, for 2 to 3 minutes, until crisp-tender.

Add the chives and lemon juice and serve immediately.

Sweet Pea Risotto
with Saffron and Parmesan

4 servings

5 to 6 cups low-salt chicken stock
¼ teaspoon saffron threads
1 tablespoon unsalted butter
1 teaspoon olive oil
¼ cup finely chopped shallot
1½ cups Arborio rice
Salt and freshly ground black pepper
¾ cup fresh peas, cooked until tender
¼ cup freshly grated Parmesan
3 tablespoons finely chopped fresh flat-leaf parsley

Combine the stock and saffron in a medium saucepan and bring to a simmer; keep warm.

In a heavy, medium saucepan, warm the butter and oil over low heat. Add the shallot and cook, stirring often, for 7 minutes, until pale golden. Add the rice, raise the heat to medium, and cook, stirring, for about 3 minutes, until the rice turns a shiny, bright white.

Add enough of the stock (about ½ cup) to barely cover the rice, and cook, stirring, until the stock is absorbed. Continue to cook in this manner, adding the stock in ½-cup increments and waiting until it is absorbed before adding more, until the rice is creamy but still al dente; the whole process will take about 20 minutes. Toward the end, taste for salt and pepper. Add the peas with the final half-cup of stock.

Remove the risotto from the heat, stir in the Parmesan and parsley, and serve immediately.

spring *fruits*

The delicate, fragrant fruits of spring–velvety apricots, juicy cherries, tart rhubarb, and sweet strawberries–are so naturally lush-tasting that they need minimal cooking and few embellishments, resulting in desserts that are lighter and simpler than the more substantial, complexly flavored desserts made with winter fruits.

In creating the recipes that follow, I let the freshest, ripest fruits be the stars and amplified their flavors with simple complementary seasonings like vanilla, ginger, nutmeg, and lemon zest, adding textural contrast with crisp almonds and amaretti, silken vanilla sauce, and creamy mascarpone.

a p r i c o t s

Because apricots are among the first tree fruits to ripen, the Romans called them *praecocia*, meaning "precocious," which later became "apricots." Like peaches, plums, cherries, and almonds, they belong to the rose family, and apricot pits do taste almondy—as anyone who has eaten amaretti cookies, of which they are a primary ingredient, will attest. Their botanical affinity to almonds also explains apricots' culinary affinity to them. One of the great gustatory pleasures of spring is a perfectly ripe apricot with some almonds and a mild fresh cheese like mascarpone, ricotta, or fromage blanc.

Apricots are very delicate and must be picked by hand. Their season in California, where 96 percent of our crop comes from, starts in mid-May and lasts eight weeks. The state of Washington also grows apricots, with a later season running from late June to mid-August.

Buying Criteria Good apricots are hard to find, largely because they are often picked unripe and don't get a chance to develop their full flavor. Look for plump, nicely shaped apricots with no green tinge or bruises. They should give slightly to the touch, like a ripe avocado, but not feel mushy. The best indication of flavor, as with any fruit, is aroma, so be sure to smell the stem end.

To Prepare for Cooking To peel apricots, simply plunge them into boiling water for 10 seconds, then run under cold water, and remove the skins with your finger or a small knife.

Warm Apricots
with Mascarpone and Amaretti

4 servings

I love this combination of warm, sweet-tart fruit and cold creamy mascarpone. If mascarpone is unavailable, substitute crème fraîche. Try this with peaches or nectarines when summer comes.

Preheat the broiler.

In a small bowl, gently toss the apricots with the butter, vanilla, Cognac, and sugar.

Arrange the apricots, cut-sides-down, on a broiler pan and cook on the middle rack of the broiler for 5 minutes, or until flecked with brown.

Let the apricots cool to warm. Put four halves on each plate, and fill the center of each with a dab of mascarpone. Top the cheese with a sprinkling of amaretti crumbs.

8 ripe apricots, peeled, halved, and pitted

4 teaspoons unsalted butter, melted

1 tablespoon vanilla extract

1 tablespoon Cognac

4 teaspoons sugar, or more if the apricots are very tart

2 tablespoons mascarpone, cold

3 tablespoons crumbled amaretti cookies

Rustic Apricot Tart with Almonds

6 servings

Serve this with crème Anglaise or honey-vanilla ice cream.

To make the Pâte Sucrée, combine the flour, butter, sugar, and salt in the work bowl of a food processor and pulse about eight times, or until the butter pieces are the size of large peas. Add 2 tablespoons of the water, sprinkling it over the flour mixture, and process for 3 seconds. Transfer to a lightly floured surface. If the dough seems dry, add a little more water—just enough to hold it together when pressed. Toss the mixture with your hands to incorporate the water, then blend by pushing the dough down and away from you with the heels of your hands, working in sections. Streaks or pieces of the butter should still be visible. Form into a thick disk, cover with plastic wrap, and flatten a bit more. Refrigerate for a minimum of 1 hour, or overnight (the dough also freezes well).

Before rolling out the dough, let it sit for 5 minutes, then roll it out into an 11- or 12-inch circle. Transfer to a baking sheet, cover with plastic wrap, and chill for 10 minutes or so, until firm.

Pâte Sucrée

1 cup all-purpose flour

7 tablespoons frozen unsalted butter, cut into 28 pieces

2 teaspoons sugar

⅛ teaspoon salt

2 to 3 tablespoons ice water, approximately

Filling

**8 medium ripe apricots,
about 3 ounces each,
peeled, halved, and pitted**

**1 tablespoon vanilla
extract**

**2 tablespoons sugar, or
more if the apricots are
very tart** ·

**1 tablespoon unsalted
butter**

½ cup sliced almonds

**Confectioners' sugar for
dusting**

While the dough chills, gently toss the apricots in a bowl with the vanilla and sugar. Preheat the oven to 400° F.

Leaving a 1-inch border, arrange the apricot halves, cut-sides-down, in concentric circles on the dough, keeping them close together. Fold the border in to make a crust, pressing down lightly. Decorate with the tines of a fork, or flute, if you're so inclined. Dot the butter over the apricot halves.

Bake in the middle of the oven for 15 minutes, then sprinkle with the almonds and cook until deep golden, about 20 minutes longer, moving the tart to the upper rack for the last 10 minutes. Immediately transfer the tart from the baking sheet to a cooling rack.

Serve warm, not hot, dusted with confectioners' sugar.

sweet cherries

Another member of the rose family is the sweet cherry, which has a season that always seems too short for me—from mid-June to early August. Most of the U.S. crop comes from the Northwest and Rocky Mountain states of Washington, Oregon, Idaho, and Utah, which have the distinct microclimate necessary to grow cherries—a microclimate so specific that cherries can be grown in limited areas of only twenty countries in the world. Most of the cherries grown in this country are red, of which Bing is the best-known variety. In recent years, however, Queen Ann or Royal Ann cherries, which are yellow with a rosy or orange tinge, have begun to appear in produce markets. They are similar in flavor to the red varieties and look lovely, but I find them to be a little softer and not as intensely flavored.

My favorite way to eat cherries is out of hand and in great quantities—red-stained hands and nails be damned—but like apricots, they go well with almonds and mild fresh cheeses. They are, of course, great in pies, sauces, and compotes, but to my taste, the less you fuss with them, the better they are.

Buying Criteria The sweetest red cherries tend to be shiny, dark in color, and very firm. For both red and Queen Ann cherries, choose unblemished specimens, and if your greengrocer is willing (or if you're sneaky), sample one or two.

To Prepare for Cooking Remove the stems and pit with a cherry pitter or by cutting the cherry in half with a small knife and twisting the pit out.

Bob's Cherry Pie with Vanilla Sauce

8 servings

Like most people who grew up eating the overcooked, gloppy, corn-starch-laden ones sold at diners, I'd never had a good cherry pie—until I tasted this extraordinary version made by Bob Hoebee, one of the finest chefs and bakers I know.

Vanilla Sauce
- 1 cup milk
- 1 small vanilla bean or 1 tablespoon vanilla extract
- 3 large egg yolks
- 3½ tablespoons sugar

Buttery Pâte Sucrée
- 3 cups all-purpose flour
- 6 tablespoons sugar
- 2 teaspoons salt
- 14 ounces (1¾ cups) chilled unsalted butter, cut into ½-inch chunks
- 6 to 8 tablespoons ice water

To make the Vanilla Sauce, combine the milk and vanilla bean, if using, in a saucepan. Bring the milk to a simmer, remove from the heat, cover, and let steep for 15 minutes. Scrape the seeds from the vanilla bean into the milk with a small knife and reserve the vanilla bean pod. In a medium bowl, beat the egg yolks with the sugar by hand or with an electric mixer until thick and lemon-colored. Stir a third of the milk into the yolks to temper them, then slowly beat in the remaining milk. Cook in the top of a double boiler, stirring, until the sauce coats the back of a wooden spoon (165° F. on a candy thermometer). Strain the sauce into a bowl, stir in the vanilla

Filling

**12 cups (2¾ pounds)
  cherries, pitted**
**1 lemon, juice squeezed
  and zest removed in long
  strips with a vegetable
  peeler**
**1¼ cups plus 2 tablespoons
  sugar**
**1 vanilla bean, split length-
  wise, or 2 tablespoons
  vanilla extract**
**2 tablespoons all-purpose
  flour**
**2 tablespoons unsalted
  butter**

extract, if using, or return the vanilla bean pod to the sauce to flavor it further as it chills. Cover the surface of the sauce with plastic wrap to prevent a film from forming. Refrigerate for several hours or overnight.

Make the Buttery Pâte Sucrée, following the technique on page 94. Divide the dough into two rounds, one slightly larger than the other, flatten into thick disks, and cover with plastic wrap. Refrigerate for at least 1 hour, then remove the larger round from the refrigerator and roll out on a lightly floured surface to a 12-inch circle. Line a 9-inch pie pan with the pastry, cover, and chill. Roll out the smaller disk of dough to an 11-inch circle, cover with plastic wrap, and refrigerate while you prepare the filling.

Preheat the oven to 450° F. Line a baking sheet with foil and place it in the oven; this will help to brown the bottom crust and catch any juices. Mix a third of the cherries with the lemon zest, 1¼ cups sugar, and vanilla bean or extract in a saucepan. Cover and cook for 5 minutes over medium heat. Remove the lid and cook for 25 to 30 minutes longer, or until the mixture thickens and resembles cherry jam. Remove from the heat, discarding the lemon zest and vanilla bean, if used. Cool slightly, then add the remaining raw cherries, plus the lemon juice and flour.

Pour into the pie shell and dot the filling with the butter. Cover with the smaller round of pastry and crimp the crusts together to seal. Make a few slits with a small knife in the top crust. Put a band of foil around the edges of the crust; this will keep the top crust from sliding off as the butter melts during cooking. Remove the foil halfway through the baking time.

Put the pie on the foil-lined baking sheet and bake for 10 minutes. Reduce the heat to 350° F. and bake for 30 minutes longer. Sprinkle the top with the remaining 2 tablespoons of sugar to glaze it, and bake for 10 minutes longer, until golden. Serve warm or at room temperature with the Vanilla Sauce.

Crisp Ricotta Pancakes
with Warm Cherry Compote

2 servings

These pancakes are wonderful—kind of like ricotta cheese with a thin, crisp crust. The compote can be made ahead and reheated for serving. Try this for dessert or brunch.

Combine all the compote ingredients in a small, heavy, nonreactive saucepan. Bring to a boil and cook over low heat for 10 minutes, stirring often, until the cherries have softened. Remove the cherries and lemon zest with a slotted spoon and transfer to a bowl; discard the zest. Reduce the juices over medium-high heat for 2 minutes, until syrupy, and pour over the cherries. Set aside or refrigerate.

Cherry Compote

½ pound cherries, pitted and coarsely chopped
1 tablespoon sugar
1 strip lemon zest, about 1 x 1½ inches
4 teaspoons red wine (I like Côtes du Rhône, Merlot, or zinfandel)
1 tablespoon water

To make the pancakes, whisk the egg yolk, ricotta, and butter in a medium bowl until combined. Whisk in the remaining pancake ingredients, except the seltzer, until combined, then whisk in the seltzer. Cover and let rest at room temperature for 30 minutes.

In a nonstick skillet over medium heat, melt enough butter to film the bottom of the pan. When the foam subsides, drop the batter by tablespoons, spreading each

Ricotta Pancakes

1 large egg yolk
½ cup ricotta (use super-
  market, rather than
  Italian deli type, which is
  too moist for this)
2 teaspoons unsalted
  butter, melted, cooled
  slightly
4 teaspoons sifted all-
  purpose flour
1½ teaspoons sugar
¼ teaspoon vanilla extract
Tiny pinch salt
Freshly grated nutmeg to
  taste
4 teaspoons seltzer

Additional butter for cook-
  ing the pancakes
Confectioners' sugar for
  dusting

mound of batter slightly. Cook for about 2 minutes on the first side, 1 on the second, until browned; turn carefully—they are quite delicate. If necessary, cook in batches, keeping the pancakes warm in a 150° F. oven until all are done. You should end up with eight small pancakes.

If necessary, reheat the cherry compote. Place four pancakes on each plate, overlapping slightly. Spoon some of the cherry compote across them in a line, and sprinkle with the confectioners' sugar.

r h u b a r b

Known familiarly as pie plant, rhubarb is botanically a vegetable, being made up of stalks and leaves, but was officially designated a fruit in 1947 by no less an authority than the U.S. Customs Court in Buffalo—one of the saner decisions the government has made, since rhubarb (in this country, at least) is used most often as a fruit.

Most of our rhubarb crop comes from Washington, California, Oregon, Michigan, and New York, and Utica, Michigan, has named itself the "Rhubarb Capital of the World." Supplies are most plentiful in May and June.

Naturally tart rhubarb is wonderful in compotes, as a dessert sauce, or in coffeecakes and tea breads, and is, of course, classically paired with strawberries in pies and tarts. Vanilla and ginger taste delicious with rhubarb, complementing and heightening its taste without being intrusive.

Rhubarb leaves contain a harmful amount of oxalic acid (also contained in the stalks, but in safer quantities) and should never be eaten.

Buying Criteria Buy rhubarb as you would celery, choosing firm, unblemished specimens with perky, fresh-looking leaves and no signs of browning. Color is no indication of flavor, as it can range from greenish-red to scarlet, depending on the growing conditions, with warmer temperatures producing greener fruit.

To Prepare for Cooking Discard the leaves. If the rhubarb seems stringy when you cut it, simply pull off the strings, as you would with celery.

Rhubarb-Vanilla Sauce

6 servings

Serve this pretty pink sauce with ice cream (vanilla and strawberry are particularly good) or sorbet.

Put all of the ingredients in a heavy saucepan. Bring to a simmer and cook, stirring occasionally, over low heat, for 15 minutes, or until the rhubarb pieces have begun to dissolve.

Remove the vanilla bean, split it down the middle, and with a small knife, scrape the seeds back into the sauce. Break up any remaining chunks of rhubarb with a spoon. For a sauce with a bit of texture and a rustic look, leave as is; for a smooth sauce, put the mixture through a food mill fitted with the medium disk.

Cool or refrigerate before serving.

Note: You can substitute 1 teaspoon vanilla extract for the bean, adding it once the sauce has finished cooking.

¾ pound rhubarb, cut into 1-inch pieces
⅓ cup sugar
1 tablespoon water
One 2-inch piece vanilla bean (see Note)
Tiny pinch salt

Gingered Rhubarb Upside-Down Cake

6 to 8 servings

Most upside-down cakes are too high and clunky-looking for me. This one is only as high as a layer cake, with a more refined look and just the right proportion of fruit to cake. It's a good dessert for a simple supper or brunch, served plain or warm with some crème fraîche or ice cream.

Gingered Rhubarb

4 tablespoons (½ stick) unsalted butter

3 cups ¼-inch-thick rhubarb slices

1 cup light brown sugar, lightly packed

½-inch piece ginger root, peeled

To make the Gingered Rhubarb, combine all of the ingredients in a large skillet and cook, stirring often, over medium-high heat for 10 minutes, or until the rhubarb is tender and a light syrup has formed. Remove the rhubarb to a bowl with a slotted spoon, discard the ginger, and reduce the juices over high heat, stirring, about 3 minutes, until thick enough to coat the back of a wooden spoon. Immediately remove from the heat, combine with the reserved rhubarb, and spread evenly over the bottom of a buttered 9-inch round cake pan.

Preheat the oven to 350° F.

To make the cake, sift the dry ingredients together in a large bowl. In a separate bowl with an electric mixer on medium speed, cream the butter and sugar with the vanilla for 2 minutes, until

Cake

1 cup sifted all-purpose flour
¼ teaspoon baking soda
¼ teaspoon baking powder
⅛ teaspoon salt
6 tablespoons (¾ stick) unsalted butter, softened
½ cup sugar
1 teaspoon vanilla extract
2 large egg yolks
½ cup buttermilk

fluffy. With the mixer on low speed, add the egg yolks, one at a time, until they are incorporated. Add the dry ingredients and buttermilk alternately, half of each at a time, and mix just until combined, scraping the bowl as needed.

Pour the batter over the rhubarb and carefully spread it evenly to the edges. Put the pan on a baking sheet and bake for 40 minutes, until the center of the cake springs back when touched.

Cool the cake on a rack (still in the pan) for 1 hour, then run a dinner knife or frosting spatula around the edges of the cake to loosen it. Place a plate over the pan, then invert the cake onto the plate.

strawberries

Except for those poor souls who are allergic to them, it seems that just about everyone likes strawberries. Happily, strawberries have an inordinately long growing season, with the first berries ripening in San Diego and Orange counties, California, as early as late January, and the last, from the Watsonville/Salinas area of California, in November. The peak season is April, May, and June for California berries, June for most other parts of the country.

Wild strawberries, which the French call *fraises des bois* ("forest strawberries"), are tiny, sweet, and usually expensive because they are almost as fragile to handle as raspberries. Look for them at farmers' markets, where they tend to be fresher and more reasonably priced.

Because of their fairly high water content, strawberries taste best raw or macerated, rather than cooked. They are delicious served with sweet cream, lightly sweetened sour cream, mascarpone, crème fraîche, or—my favorite—Devon cream, which is sold at many specialty food stores and supermarkets. Slice strawberries and macerate them with a little sugar and vanilla and serve over ice cream, or melt some good bittersweet chocolate and dip the berries in it as a fondue (when eaten immediately) or a confection (when the chocolate coating is allowed to harden, making a thin crisp shell); long-stemmed berries are particularly impressive for dipping. For an easy, fresh-tasting dessert, do as the Italians do: sprinkle strawberries with a little balsamic vinegar. Mint, chocolate, vanilla, orange, red wine, and the various berry-flavored eaux-de-vie are good flavor complements to strawberries.

Buying Criteria Your nose should be your primary guide when choosing strawberries; if they have no aroma, they will have no taste, either. Many markets sell berries wrapped in plastic, which makes the aroma test impossible; shop elsewhere. Strawberries do not continue to ripen after picking, so choose aromatic, firm ones with a rich red color and fresh-looking green caps, avoiding those with white or green areas, bruises, or soft spots.

To Prepare for Cooking Just before serving or cooking, remove the green caps and hull after a brief rinse in cold water. Whole, unhulled berries look lovely as part of a fruit platter or as garnish for sorbets, ice cream, and chocolate desserts.

My Kind of Strawberry Shortcake

6 servings

Strawberry shortcake was my mother's favorite dessert, but I never could work up much enthusiasm for the kind we used to buy at our neighborhood bakery in Brooklyn, with its soft yellow cake and bland, fluffy whipped cream—it always seemed like baby food to me. It wasn't until years later, when I tasted real strawberry shortcake made with a biscuity dough, that I became a convert. I've experimented with many recipes since then, and I like this one best. The shortcake has a tender crumb like a cake but is crisp and buttery like a biscuit.

Toss the strawberries in a small bowl with the sugar and vanilla and refrigerate, covered, for at least 1 hour, so that the fruit juices and dissolved sugar form a kind of sauce. Remove from the refrigerator about 15 minutes before serving to take the chill off.

3 cups sliced strawberries
1 tablespoon sugar
1 teaspoon vanilla extract

To make the shortcake, preheat the oven to 400° F. Sift together the dry ingredients in a bowl. Add the butter and, with a pastry blender or the tips of your fingers, rub it into the dry ingredients until the butter is the size of small peas. Stir in the cream and buttermilk until just combined; the dough will be sticky. Turn out onto a lightly floured sur-

Shortcake

2 cups sifted all-purpose
   flour
2½ teaspoons baking
   powder
½ teaspoon baking soda
½ teaspoon salt
4 teaspoons sugar
4 tablespoons (½ stick)
   cold unsalted butter, cut
   into bits
⅞ cup heavy cream
¼ cup buttermilk

Egg Wash

1 large egg yolk
1 tablespoon heavy cream

½ cup heavy cream
1 teaspoon superfine sugar
Mint sprigs

face, and with floured hands, knead four or five times, just until the dough is no longer sticky. Roll or pat the dough into a ¾-inch-thick rectangle, and with a floured 3-inch biscuit cutter, cut out circles as close together as possible. You will have extra dough scraps, but don't be tempted to reroll them; they will be a bit tough when baked.

Transfer the shortcakes to an ungreased baking sheet, placing the rounds 1 inch apart. With a fork, beat the egg yolk with the cream until blended, and brush over the top and sides of each shortcake. Bake for 20 minutes, until golden. Transfer to a cooling rack and cool thoroughly.

Beat the cream to soft peaks, adding the sugar when it is whipped halfway.

To serve, cut each shortcake in half with a serrated knife. Spoon some berries on the bottom half, add some whipped cream, then replace the top half, add a spoonful of berries, and garnish each plate with mint sprigs.

Strawberry Gratin

4 servings

I've always loved toasted marshmallows, with their sweet, soft insides and burnt sugar crust. This tastes like a sophisticated, strawberry-flavored version of that campfire treat. For a more elegant presentation, cook this gratin in individual ramekins.

3 large egg yolks
7 teaspoons sugar
¼ cup dry Marsala
¼ teaspoon (rounded) finely grated orange zest
1 pint strawberries, stemmed, hulled, sliced fairly thin
¼ cup toasted sliced almonds

Have ready a double boiler bottom or medium saucepan partly filled with simmering water. Preheat the broiler.

In the top of the double boiler, off-heat, or in a stainless-steel bowl that will fit over the saucepan, beat together the egg yolks and sugar with a whisk or electric beater until slightly thickened. Stir in the Marsala and zest and put the bowl over, not in, the simmering water. Cook for a few minutes, whisking constantly, until as thick as a cream sauce. Remove from the heat.

Arrange the berries in a gratin dish just large enough to hold them in a shallow layer, and pour the sauce over the top. Cook under the broiler on the middle rack for 4 minutes, until browned. Sprinkle with the almonds and serve immediately.

i n d e x